UNIQUE THINKING

Leading and Managing by Thoughts

SRILEKHA KALUVAKUNTA

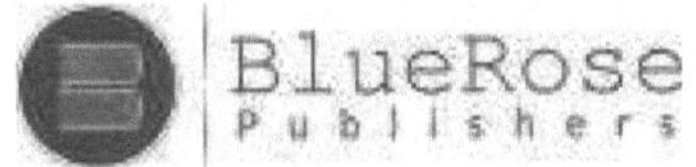

First Published in June 2021

ISBN: 978-93-5427-721-4

BLUEROSE PUBLISHERS

www.bluerosepublishers.com

info@bluerosepublishers.com

+91 8882 898 898

Cover Design:

Ayona Tomar

Typographic Design:

Deepika Matpal

Distributed by: BlueRose, Amazon, Flipkart

UNIQUE THINKING

(Leading and Managing by Thoughts)

Thought Management for Uniqueness in Thinking and Unique Thought Process

One of the best thought management leadership and execution guides for success that can change the way you Think

How this book can change the way you think

Unique Thinking is one of the best thought management leadership and execution guides that can change the way we think by defining the ways of thinking unique and different; focused on methods and practices to attain these unique thinking capabilities. It covers the concepts of how we need to think in order to achieve the desired results we want and fulfill our aspirations and dreams by way of our thoughts and thought process. It details about how we can change our life by our thoughts to get results just by changing the ways of our thought process.

You think unique that is when you act unique and that is when you become unique and distinguished among your colleagues, friends and family.

This book Unique Thinking can direct the ways of our thoughts and thought process and illustrates how we can manage our mind and thoughts during the mental states of ambiguity and distraction. It is focused on the concepts of Thought Management for attaining the states of Uniqueness in Thinking and Unique Thought Process.

About the Author

I was interested in analyzing about the concepts of thinking unique, thought management, leadership, thought execution and mind control from my childhood and was more inclined towards understanding management of thoughts and thought leadership aspects of it and always wondered how our thoughts influence our life. I had several personal observations for the reason and impact of the changes in the ways of our thinking and thought process in our life. I started my analysis and study about these concepts by interacting with various groups of people from different backgrounds and professions which included spiritual people and masters in meditation practices.

My family and friends helped me in my analysis and study about thoughts; because of whom I had come across various situations and circumstances in life, interact with different groups of people and got to know many things for myself through my personal experiences; this paved a path for my understanding about how thoughts impact our life; by changing the ways of thinking how can we change our life and situations and how unique thinking can have distinguished impact on a person's life.

Along with this many other factors made me materialize my analysis, observations and study in the form a book that you are reading now.

Sincerely, Lekha(Pinky)

Contents

1

Introduction to Unique Thinking

Before I start talking about Unique Thinking I would like to question myself

What is a Thought?

Many of us are not exactly clear about the definition of a thought even though we hear it almost every day

In this book, we will know about thoughts; methods and practices to manage thoughts; indepth analysis and details about uniqueness of thoughts and newly designed concepts of Management Thinking Objectives (MTO) that describe Unique Thought Process (UTP) and real time examples and scenarios connected with Thought Lifecycle Management (TLM)

We all know that the thoughts are powerful whether positive or negative and we need to design our thinking very carefully in order to be successful and to get what we want.

So, What makes a Thought so powerful?

How can we manage the way we Think?

According to me, a Thought is what distinguishes a person because thinking varies from person to person.

A Thought creates an identity to a person.

A Thought is what we live in everyday.

A Thought is what we execute everyday.

A Thought is what makes us.

A Thought is what makes our life.

According to the scientific definition of a Thought, it is the neuro electrical signal generated by the brain based on our five sensory perceptions.

To be precise and not to be too elaborative on the scientific definition of what a Thought is all about, speaking in a day to day context,

A Thought is a goal oriented flow of ideas resulting in reality oriented conclusion.

A Thought is an idea or opinion produced by Thinking or sudden occurrence in the mind.

What is Thought Management?

I got a Thought about this Thought Management when I was thinking about What is a Thought and what makes a Thought so powerful and how Thoughts can be controlled and managed.

A Thought put into action is what distinguishes a Dream from Reality.

Organization of Thoughts make any activity or work a success or failure in life.

Can we say that a Thought decides our success or failure in life?

As we all desire success in life, how do we organize our Thoughts so as to achieve the desired expected outcome.

This is what I Thought, to be called as Management of Thoughts for attaining Uniqueness In Thinking (UIT) and establishing with our mind the Unique Thought Process (UTP) and Thought Lifecycle Management (TLM)

What is a DREAM?

A DREAM can be defined as the recollection of Thoughts that happened in the past or the vision of Thoughts that will happen in the Future.

2

Concepts of Uniqueness in Thinking and Unique Thought Process

Management Objectives of Thinking (MTO) focuses on managing our Thoughts in such a way so as to achieve the expected results; motivate and inspire others to enhance and improve their abilities and capabilities; both in personal and professional environment.

The main focus of this book is concentrated on the applicability of the Unique Thinking and concepts of Uniqueness of Thoughts both in Personal and Professional arena that can change the way we think and the way we live.

A Thought stands as a distinguishing criteria of a person

I believe a Thought distinguishes between an experienced person and an inexperienced person, a Boss, a Manager and a Leader.

So, I believe managing and leading by way of Uniqueness in Thinking and Unique Thought Process which I acronym it as UIT and UTP has got a considerable importance at work place.

Uniqueness in Thinking UIT

As we have already seen how a Thought stands as a distinguishing criteria among people; Uniqueness in Thinking creates an identity and recognition to a person among his/her family, peers, colleagues and friends.

So, the very next Thought that comes to our mind in the form of a question is how do we think in a unique way?

And What is called Uniqueness?

When I was thinking about this, a Thought flashed through my mind as to why cannot we think unique?

And I define Uniqueness as our very own nature and ways of Thinking and acting upon anything or any given situation.

The scientific origin of human beings itself says that no two people look alike and behave exactly similar. Even for the infants born as Twins that took birth from the mother's womb at the same time, there are differences in the way they think, the way they behave and the way they react to surroundings and situations.

Similarly, ***Thought Process*** also differs from Person to Person. That means every one of us is gifted with the uniqueness in resemblance and Thinking at the time of birth itself.

But as we gradually grow, we tend to lose our gift of uniqueness looking at other people, our surroundings, the way people behave and react to situations; that is we grow up imitating others knowingly or unknowingly and never bother to think about our unique qualities and capabilities hidden within us; because we don't have enough time to spend for ourselves and think about ourselves which is the most common thing with almost everyone of us.

Experiment with your thoughts on a fine weekend:

On a pleasant weekend when the weather is good and the mind is free from unorganized Thoughts and tensions (we'll see about organized thinking in the next chapter).

Think about yourself as to who you are; what you want to become; what makes you happy and What makes the person you are today.

After all the unorganized and clumsy thinking, you get to the state where you start to feel that Yes! This is what I like or this is what I feel like doing or This is the Person I am or the Person I want to be.

And that *Thought* distinguishes you from others and that creates your *Uniqueness Quotient.*

These unique qualities hidden within us when we try to execute them in our life make us stand out unique and this process of realizing the potential hidden within us by way of thinking and perceiving about any given situation or surroundings is what is called Uniqueness in Thinking UIT

Unique Thought Process UTP

Every individual's mind is engaged with Thoughts which take the form of actions that define our identity and recognition of a person.

So can we say that a Thought defines the Work Process of a Person?

A Thought is a sudden occurrence in the mind based on our five sensory perceptions.

What defines a Thought Process?

We need to know that our Thoughts will go through various stages during Thought Life Cycle of a person.

Stages of Thought Process

1. Thought Occurrence
2. Thought Sustenance
3. Thought Realization
4. Thought Organization and Design
5. Thought Execution
6. Thought Outcome
7. Thought Reoccurrence
8. Thought Continuity
9. Thought Lapse

Thought Life Cycle

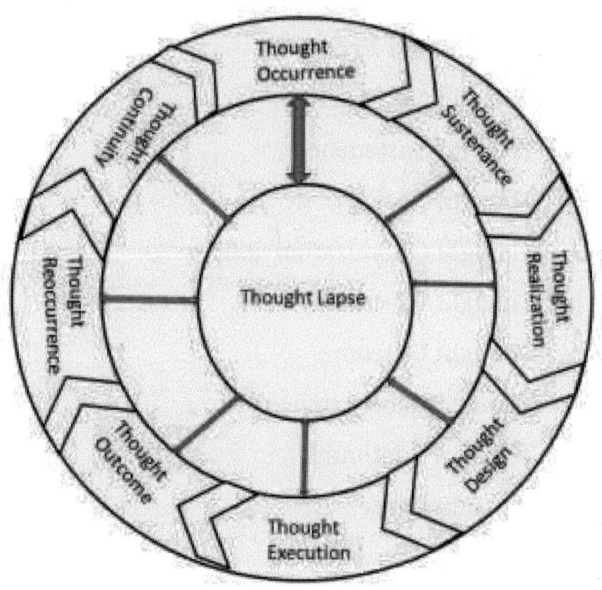

Every individual's mind traverses through these phases of the Thought which forms the **Thought Process Framework**

Thought Occurrence:

A Thought is an idea generated in the mind as a result of the stimulation from the surroundings or people surrounding us; or can be defined as a sudden recollection of our knowledge and experiences.

This Occurrence of Thought is the initial phase of the Thought Process which stands as the starting point in the Unique Thought Process.

All of us get Thoughts every single second but they don't sustain in our minds or we don't remember what we think most of the times.

For these type of non-sustaining thoughts which don't have any impact on our Thought Process, Thought Occurrence and Thought Lapse stages occur consecutively one after the other.

Thought Sustenance:

Thought Sustenance forms the next stage of Thought Occurrence and only sustained thoughts enter this stage. We can consider it as the initiation of the Thought Process and Thought Management Life Cycle.

These sustained thoughts which we call it as ideas form the distinguishing **Factor of Change** in our life.

Thought Realization:

These sustained Thoughts move to the Thought Realization phase where we feel our ideas to be considered worthy and we feel like taking them forward and executing them. That feeling of importance we give to our ideas and thoughts is called Thought Realization.

Thought Organization and Design:

After we realize our thoughts, we tend to structure or organize our thoughts as per our requirements using some inferences of our surroundings, images, audio and video messages, our experiences and knowledge.

That means we are designing our Thoughts based on our needs and requirements.

Thought Execution:

After we structure our Thoughts in the required manner, we go with executing our Thought Design. This is when we take some action against our Thoughts to achieve the desired expected outcome.

Thought Outcome:

Thought Outcome is the result of the Thought Execution. So, Thought Design and Thought Execution form the key deciding factors for success or failure in life.

Thought Reoccurrence:

Thought Reoccurrence is the stage where we will be able to recollect all the previous thoughts clearly that have lead to the Thought Outcome which decide the result of any work or activity we do. So, Thought Execution forms the most important stage of the Thought Process.

Thought Continuity:

Thought Continuity is the phase wherein we get the flow of ideas or thoughts that help us achieve the expected outcome.

Thought Continuity can be a continuous process or it can start from Thought Occurrence for subsequent ideas and thoughts.

This phase continues until the expected outcome is achieved.

Thought Lapse:

Thought Lapse is the final stage of the Thought Process wherein we tend to forget our Thoughts and the Thought Process Cycle tends to fade away gradually with time and active engagement of our mind in other activities in life.

Consisting of the phases of the Thought from Thought Occurrence till Thought Lapse; this Thought Process forms the Thought Process Life Cycle and this forms the Unique Thought Process UTP

Thought Lapse replaces with the generation of the new thought and thus Thought Process Lifecycle is a continuous process that happens constantly in everyone's mind without one's knowledge.

Distinguished Thinking and the Difference of Thinking from others; this way of execution of the Thought Process forms the Unique Thought Process UTP

3

Organized Thinking Vs Unorganized Thinking

Organized Thinking can be defined as a structured way of Thinking.

From an unlimited pool of ideas and thoughts, the way we organize the thoughts relevant for our requirements so as to achieve the expected outcome forms the concept of Organized Thinking.

Organized Thinking is all about how we can sequentially organize or prioritize or execute the elements of a Thought in a structure or hierarchy of Thought Process.

This universe is made of energy and matter and Thought can be defined as the conversion of Energy into signals based on a particular frequency with which it vibrates at that level; which in turn creates the manifestation of images and vision upon thinking continuously will get materialized into Reality that we can see.

As we understand, Thought is not a physical entity that we can see but what we see is the manifestation of Thought materialized into Reality.

Organized Thinking forms a significant phenomenon in the concept of Law of Thinking.

Law of Thinking states that everything we see in Reality is the result of the materialization of the Manifested Visions and Thoughts.

Organized Thinking is the grouping of ideas in a structured hierarchy which when acted upon parallelly or sequentially will result in the expected outcome.

So we can infer from this that the way we organize and design our Thoughts define success and failure in our life.

This plays a very important role in the Thought Execution process.

As we all know, we are valued based on our actions which are in turn dependent on our Thoughts.

How do we structure and organize our Thoughts so as to achieve the results or success we all dream about?

This is what forms the focus of the concept of Uniqueness of Thoughts that defines how we can manage and control our Thoughts to meet our own needs and expectations.

To attain Organized Thinking, we need to initially attain a Positive Mindset.

Memories

If the frequency of our Thoughts match with the frequency of Manifested Thoughts that were materialized in the past, we will be able to recollect those incidents or Thoughts which we call as Memories.

Visions

If the frequency of our thoughts match with the frequency of incidents that are going to take place in Future, we get the vision of those incidents.

In general terms, we call it as Sixth Sense or Intuition or Inner voice. We hear about this quite often from the people around us, but we never try to analyze what causes that intuition in us all of sudden pertaining to a certain context.

We can remember past memories only if those incidents had a very strong impact on one's life or one's self that those thoughts get stored in the subconscious mind and manifest in the present in the form of memories; like how the images are captured and stored in the memory card in camera.

Belief

Belief can be defined as the Thought of our Mind that emerges from our experiences as a result of the actions in our past or events in our future.

Organized Thinking defines as to how we like to act upon any situation or how we like to lead our life.

Everybody has a defined goal as to where they want to reach in life or how to lead their life that forms the criteria for organized thinking for that person.

Organized Thinking forms the mindset of a person.

A psychologically organized person will have the uniqueness of his thoughts and not just follow people who come across unlike with an unorganized person with unorganized Thought Process.

An organized person will have clarity of his Thoughts and Actions while the unorganized person will have a clumsy, distractive and a confusing mindset.

An organized person will have confidence in what he believes and focused thoughts to work towards achieving his dreams and goals.

An organized person with Positive Mindset will be flowing with Positive attitude and Positive energy.

Our Thoughts define our actions that create the identity of a person. A person with Positive mindset can be easily distinguished from a person with a negative state of mind.

People with Positive Thinking and Positive attitude will not only create identity for themselves but also influence others in getting inspired from them and provide an opportunity to learn from their life and experiences.

A Person with positive mindset always tries to offer help to others in whichever way possible and stands out amongst other people in the group; because his thoughts are organized that result in his actions and he will have control on his mind unlike an unorganized person who lacks control of himself and his actions.

All the successful people in this world must have mastered the art of Positive Thinking and have complete control on their Thoughts and Mind. They have learnt to design their Thoughts in an organized way that resulted in their actions which paved a way for their success.

Unless we have clarity of our own thoughts, we will not be achieving things we desire for. This is the proven statement of the Thought Management because as long as we don't have clarity in thinking, we will not be working towards anything as our mind will not have a **direction of thinking.**

First we need to state our mind what we want and then ask it how to achieve it and then program it with the required information and knowledge and then allow it to work for us.

This relates to the concept of Subconscious mind and Conscious way of Thinking.

Subconscious mind is like the creative and innovative mind from where new thoughts get generated.

This is the invisible mind that forms the mapping of our visible mind with the universal oneness of mind.

There are many popular books written on the working and miracles of the subconscious mind. But unique thinking altogether takes a different approach for understanding about the thoughts and mind.

(We will see the concepts of universal mind and oneness of mind in chapter10).

Organized Thinking is a phenomenon where we tend to sequentially organize our thoughts with a specific goal in mind that leads to the expected outcome.

Our mind will get the abundant data available in the universal library specific to our goals and expectations; all that we need to do is organize and design our thought process based on our needs.

This forms the major difference between a person with an organized mindset and a person with unorganized mindset.

A Person with Organized Thought Process will have the knowledge and knows what to do with the data while a Person with unorganized mindset will have the data but doesn't know what to do with the data; all that you need to learn is master the art of training your mind for listening to your commands and control it for behaving as you want;

We are already living in an abundant pool of knowledge and once we fetch the data from universal library; all that we need to do is to analyze the data for designing our thoughts to fulfill our wishes and dreams.

Organized Thinking is the basis of Thought Management and Unique Thinking that forms the most important criteria for attaining Uniqueness in Thinking and Unique Thought Process.

4

How can we lead and manage by Thoughts

Thinking is a repetitive and recurring process.

The frequency with which we think depends on the surroundings, our present state of mind, context and situation.

Everyone of us in our day to day lives lead and manage by Thoughts without our knowledge.

So, how can we manage ourselves and things related to us in such a way that we design our life with our thoughts to fulfill our wishes so as to live the life we desire and deserve.

This is one of the main focus areas that made me think towards the analysis of Unique Thinking and Management of Thoughts.

Everyone of us must have heard the Concepts of Thinking, Management of Thoughts and Design of Thoughts; but how many of us ever tried to understand the exact definition of this and implement the process of Unique Thinking in our personal and professional life?

We all usually tend to ignore our thoughts by default in every context unless we strongly feel the demand and necessity to execute them.

This happens with almost everyone of us everyday.

But did we ever try to sit back and think and analyze what is making us think the way we are thinking. Most of us don't like the life we are leading and some of us don't like the way we are; but we don't say it out.

Did we ever think what is making us lead our life the way we don't like or be the way we don't want to be?

Did we ever realize that we can live the way we like because it is our life and it is none other than us who has designed the life the way it is and the way we are leading and living in it

So what is making us think something and execute something and experience something else?

Why are we not able to have these parameters in synchronization and able to design and execute these elements in life and lead life the way we like

I believe this is where the leading and managing of thoughts come into picture in organizing and synchronizing our desires and opinions with our thoughts and visions to make us live the life we like.

We tend to organize and manage things at home but we never think of organizing and managing thoughts in our mind.

If we can develop and manage our thoughts in a way that is most desirable and deservable for us, I'm sure we can design our lives the way we like.

In general, we think something in mind but execute something else which states that we are not leading and managing our thoughts and actions.

We need to understand that only when we get the synchronicity between our thoughts and actions we will be able to achieve the desired outcome.

We need to have the vision stated clearly with specified objectives established to implement and execute for achieving the stated mission and goals.

We need to analyze and design our thoughts and our Thought Process in such a way that it meets the needs of our expectations and visions.

Foremost thing for this is to have the clarity of thoughts as to where we want to go and what we want to accomplish.

And then develop, design and plan our thoughts accordingly.

This is called Leading and Managing our life by Leading and Managing our Thoughts.

We develop efficiency and capabilities within us based on our thoughts and experiences in life.

5

Significance of Unique Thinking and Thought Management in Professional Context

Thoughts have a major role in designing our career.

I always wondered how a Thought can have such a significant impact in our personal and professional life.

But realized it gradually that this is the fact and thoughts do really design and decide our life.

But how is it possible?

Before we understand how thoughts design and decide our life, it is very important to note what makes our thoughts and what triggers the Thought Process in a person. Every thought has its unique characteristics and purpose.

We all are working may be in different professions so the thoughts may vary but the mind would remain the same if you have heard about the concept of Universal mind and Oneness of mind.

Considering the role of our thoughts and mind in our lives and this digital age of transformation we are living in, this universe is a huge library with all the knowledge and books available with it. Our minds are like the search engines to choose the kind of books those are of interest for us and those are relevant for us.

What we search depends on our Thoughts and Thought Process which means our Thoughts will trigger our actions and interests to get the data we want from the universal library or choose the book we like, take the applicable context, implement it and execute it.

As we have seen, Unique Thinking is the art of taking decisions that in turn specify our actions. This signifies the importance of Thought Leadership and Thought Management at work place and professional environment.

A person with good thoughts will create a better environment for the people surrounding him with his positive mannerisms and vibrations.

A person with positive mindset at workplace will influence the surroundings in a positive way by showcasing his way of positive attitude and creates a positive work culture.

Many studies have already proved that positivity at work place will improve the quality of work and productivity of the team.

Developing a positive mindset forms the most basic criteria and quality of a successful person.

If one needs to be successful in life, they need to change the way they think and behave. Because thoughts are the sources of positive or negative mind.

I say it as vice-versa here if you observe very keenly.

I don't say positive or negative mind is the source of positive or negative thoughts.

Rather I say positive and negative thoughts are the sources of positive or negative mind.

As I mentioned in one of the previous chapters, mind is a search engine which retrieves or queries the data from the universal pool of thoughts whether it is positive or negative depending on our needs and requirements.

So, if we go further in analyzing and thinking about this concept, we can understand that we are living in a pool of universal thoughts or term it as universal library; which is common for everyone of us that specifies the oneness of universe.

We are already living in an abundant pool of ideas and thoughts.

We just have to know how to query and retrieve the data and that's what we are learning.

A Positive mind attracts and selects the positive set of data available in the universal pool. Likewise, a negative mind selects and retrieves the negative set of data available in the universe; which category of data to choose or retrieve is dependent on us.

When we have trained our mind to think in a negative way, how can we expect to retrieve the positive data.

It is similar to searching in Google or Bing or any other internet based search engines;

Can we query for some data and get completely different set of data? Is it possible?

Our mind is also like the search engine querying for results and retrieving the data; We get what we search for.

All that we have to do is refine the search query if we are not getting the required results. That's all.

But most of us are not aware of this fact or tend to ignore this fact and get psychologically affected if they are not able to find or get what they desire.

So instead of allowing ourselves to wander around various places physically and mentally with a confused state of mind; which most of us are automatically programmed to do so; the option I suggest is to relax ourselves, attain the state of calmness of mind and then think towards how we can refine our queries to get the results from the universal library through our search engine mind.

So how do we do that? How do we develop our thinking in a way to get the results we want?

Organized and Structured way of Thinking, Adapting to Positive Thought Process,

Practicing Meditation, self awareness and self realization parameters help us in understanding this to a certain extent.

(Meditation and the states of Thoughtfulness and Thoughtlessness are covered in the next chapters.)

So to develop our thinking in a way to get the results we want, firstly we need to have clarity of our thoughts; what we desire and what we don't desire in life.

If we don't have this clarity of thought, our search engine mind will retrieve all the results which are required and which are not required that creates the state of confusion, distraction and ambiguity in life.

When applying this to professional context, we need to be clear about what we want

and what we want to become in life and where we want to take our career ahead.

****

Set up some goals that define your objectives and thoughts and start querying data relevant for that and you will observe that you will become closer to the results you expected in a much sooner and considerably lesser amount of time in a much easier and better way than expected.

For this you need to develop and improve your thoughts towards what you want and what you desire for; in order to change your life like how you want it to be and how you were dreaming about it.

We all dream about our career and success.

Dreams are nothing but the visions and thoughts of our inner desires that are to be materialized and manifested into Reality.

All that we need to do is think in synchronicity with our dreams

Did we ever realize that we consciously and unconsciously don't think in synchronization with our dreams?

If we had done that we could have achieved the results, we wanted much earlier.

Those who could do so, already achieved what they desired for.

People who have not realized this fact, keep wondering about how some of the most successful people are able to achieve the results they wanted and are leading their lives the way they desired for.

We must realize that DREAMS are our THOUGHTS unconsciously hidden in our mind. To get them to REALITY or ignore them is OUR CHOICE.

Try this Thought experiment on how to achieve what you dream:

One fine morning, Relax your mind and body. Regularize your breathing to attain the steady state of body and mind.

Once you reach to this state of present or calmness, start thinking about what you desire or wish for in life and what you want to become with complete clarity of mind.

Then start visualizing and dreaming about your thoughts, desires and dreams about your career and feel that positivity, enthusiasm and realness of achieving the results you desire for.

Repeat this for a few days regularly and you will start observing the change to your thoughts that will lead to your expected results.

This experiment was tested and proven to be successful for materialization and manifestation of dreams and thoughts for many people; but this requires complete focus and control on the body and mind and for attaining these higher levels of consciousness, we need to prepare our mind with our thoughts that will get us the results we want.

6

Thoughtfulness Vs Thoughtlessness

Thoughts as we have seen form the source elements of mind.

Being mindful and not being mindful (this is different from what we usually define as state of mindlessness or ignorance or lack of awareness, I will explain about it in detail in this chapter) will form the concepts of Thoughtfulness and Thoughtlessness.

Thoughtfulness is being mindful in activities and actions and Thoughtlessness is the state of not being mindful of Thoughts.

Calmness of mind or state of clarity of mind can be achieved through regular meditation practices; Self-realization and self-actualization also help in achieving the states of Thoughtfulness and Thoughtlessness.

How do we achieve the state of Thoughtfulness?

We all have come across this situation where our mind will be occupied by thoughts sometimes parallel thoughts occurring simultaneously in the mind.

This is not the state of Thoughtfulness as many of us believe rather I call it as confused state of mind OR a distracted state of mind.

Thoughtfulness is when we tend to think productive and with quality that meets the requirements of the solution we are expecting for a problem.

Thoughtfulness is the decisive and relative state of mind where we take the most important decisions of our life in a qualitative way.

Thoughtfulness generates new ideas in our mind where we reach to a state of generating new thoughts.

In simple terms, Thoughtfulness can be defined as being thoughtful rather than immersed in a large pool of thoughts.

Thoughtfulness state of mind is achieved when we are able to think productively that meets the needs of our problems and solutions to be achieved for those problems.

All of us must have studied various subjects all through our academic career and discuss various topics with our friends and family; many a times which we don't even have a count of it.

Have you ever realized how do you speak about a certain thing with somebody all of sudden?

Our mind retrieves the information and knowledge stored in our conscious mind that helps us talk about those things which we had already studied or situations we had already come across; that means our mind is unconsciously reaching to the state of Mindfulness or Thoughtfulness where it could generate or retrieve the thoughts or ideas relevant for the topic of discussion or situation.

I define this as a state of *Known Innovation* where we recollect the knowledge or retrieve the information we already have in our mind based on the situation and context we are dealing with; that means we are innovating with our available knowledge and wisdom for dealing with the situation and people as needed.

But what about the state of Unknown Thoughts or *Unknown Innovation* or Creativity which we never came across.

How do we reach to this state of Unknown Thoughtfulness?

As I have mentioned, we are living in an abundant pool of data and information and all that we need to have is the knowledge to retrieve the data.

I say that there is no question existing in this universe without an answer or no problem existing without a solution.

Achieving the state of Thoughtfulness through regular meditation practices which we also term it as Dhyana or Dhyan in Sanskrit will help in reaching to the state of mental awareness where we realize the potentiality of consciousness within and around us.

This will also lead us in understanding how to control our mind and command our mind and to get closer to the abundant pool of knowledge.

Our mind is the tool that can query the data, retrieve the data and store the data that is relevant for us.

But we need to understand the language of our mind to command our mind to behave as expected and bring the results we wanted.

For this firstly we need to understand what we are and what we want which most of us find it difficult to answer.

How many of us are aware of ourselves of what exactly we want and what exactly we are looking for?

I conducted a short survey on a group of people to understand their thought process as to what they think and what they are expecting out of their lives.

I was surprised to see the response from most of them that they are not exactly sure of it and would flow with time wherever it is or some of them replied that they don't know what they want and they cant achieve what they desire for; but surely will become something someday.

Some replied saying that they just follow what others say and what others want them to behave like or want them to live like.

I can understand that we live in a society where there might be certain rules and constraints to follow but has anybody told us that we need to live like how they are expecting us to live and behave like how they are expecting us to behave? But we consciously or unconsciously tend to follow this. I want to understand Why?

Why do we need to just follow others and behave like how they want us to behave and live like how they want us to live?

Nobody has put this restriction on us. We have put restrictions on us like this; Reason being lack of mindfulness and Thoughtfulness.

We don't have clarity of Thoughts as to what we want and what we want to become in life.

Once we are clear on this aspect, we can have clarity of our Thoughts and will be able to control and command our mind to bring in the results we want thus reaching to a state of Thoughtfulness.

We are the Masters of our Mind we need to realize this Fact.

Thoughtlessness

The word Thoughtlessness itself sounds peculiar and uncommon.

What is Thoughtlessness and how do we achieve the state of Thoughtlessness?

Thoughtlessness is considered to be one of the unique states of mind and highest levels of mind that is not so easy to achieve and master but it's not impossible.

There is no situation or state existing in this universe that cannot be achieved or impossible to achieve. All that you need to have is the knowledge about how to achieve it.

We have seen that with state of calmness of mind and clarity of mind we can achieve the State of Thoughtfulness.

Then how can we achieve the State of Thoughtlessness?

As stated earlier, Thoughtlessness is one of the highest levels of mind in which we reach to a state of calmness where there are no thoughts. This is next level higher to the level of Thoughtfulness.

In the state of Thoughtlessness, we cannot get any thoughts about anything and cannot recollect or retrieve any data.

It is the state where we can hear the sound of the universe which we call it as Silence and feel the vibrations of the universe within our mind.

A Thought is the conversion of energy into signals based on a particular frequency with which it vibrates at that point of time that creates the manifestation of images and vision upon thinking continuously will get materialized into Reality that we can see.

Everything and every particle in this universe is vibrating with a certain frequency. The frequency match of vibrations will bind the particles together.

At the decomposition of sub-atomic particles to the lowest levels of granularity, there is no matter existing but there is invisible energy that forms the universe and this is the origin of everything.

Most of us know that the sound of 'OM' or 'AMEN' is the origin of the universe but many of us don't know that there is no specific sound of OM; but there is only a state of Thoughtlessness and Vibration.

This is the purest form of energy which is also referred to as Energy Matrix.

The sound of OM when chanted vibrates at the frequency of 432 Hz which is the same vibrational frequency throughout the universe.

ONE MIND—ONE ENERGY THE POWER IS WITHIN US.

Reprogram your mind with a Unique belief system. Believe that anything is possible

Energy is self-controlled and self-monitored; nobody needs to monitor it or control it and nobody can control it as they themselves are made of energy. They can control energy only within certain limits and energy is infinite; Infinity has no beginning and no end.

Human brain is not capable of defining the origin and end of energy and infinity.

Humans can hear and see only certain things in this world with certain pixel resolution and decibels; less than which or beyond which human sensory perceptions don't support. *This doesn't mean they don't exist.*

Spiritual people and Saints who spend most of their time in meditation can reach to this highest state of mind where they can feel the purest form of energy and know about the Oneness of mind and Oneness of universe.

I have referred to multiple sources of study and several books and articles from my childhood about the concepts of energy and mind and met many spiritual people trying to understand these concepts.

This formed the most important aspects for realizing the importance of Unique Thinking in our lives and coming with the Concepts of Thought Management for Uniqueness in Thinking and Unique Thought Process.

7

Unique Dimensional Thinking for Managers and Leaders

We have seen that the concepts of Uniqueness of Thoughts—Uniqueness in Thinking UIT and Unique Thought Process UTP can be implemented at work place for achieving the desired expected results within the professional context.

Managers need to adapt to dimensional thinking strategies for leading and managing teams.

Dimensional Thinking forms one of the significant concepts of Thoughtfulness of mind. As we have seen in the previous chapter about Thoughtfulness and Thoughtlessness of mind; Dimensional Thinking forms the essence of Thought Management.

For easy understanding, it can be compared to the dimensions of a cube. Like how we can measure the volume, length, breadth and other dimensional statistics of a cube, likewise we can measure the directions of the Thought Process and determine the dimensions of our Thoughts in which direction we tend to think that suits with the group of people involved and relevant for the situation and context.

Dimensional Thinking is gaining prominence in the professional arena and in the corporate world because of its advantages proven in

leading and managing different sections of people within and across teams.

Like how there are different states of mind with state of Thoughtlessness being the highest level of mind one can achieve; there are several dimensions for Thoughts that we need to think about.

Not all people are alike and think similar. There are various groups of people from various locations and geographies who are from multi lingual and multi cultural backgrounds. In order to manage those people, we need to adapt to their thought process and establish the synchronicity of thoughts to completely understand their way of doing things and perception towards things and to make sure the message we are trying to convey is reaching to them in the right way.

We cant analyze different situations and scenarios in a similar way. We need to adapt to different dimensions of Thinking when dealing with different situations.

Our mind is programmed unknowingly and subconsciously from childhood to automatically adapt to thinking in various dimensions depending on the people we are dealing with and the situation being handled for the relevant context.

As a manager, you will be required to manage several teams which requires you to think in multiple dimensions and directions to have that connectivity for establishing the work culture within and across teams.

Work culture, team spirit and team integrity form the fundamental elements of increasing performance and productivity among teams.

As a leader you will be required not only to manage teams but also lead teams and the organization which requires you to think in various dimensions.

For this you need to have the dimensional thinking mindset where you adapt yourself to the capabilities of thinking with in-depth analysis of the situation and the people with various **directions of thought** assuming several permutations and combinations of thought process and come up with the appropriate understanding and analysis or solution to meet the needs and requirements of the business in order to achieve the defined objectives and vision.

Adapting to a dimensional thinking mindset will allow us to think and analyze a given situation or a scenario in multiple directions.

As already stated, like how a cube will have the dimensions of measurement interms of volume, length and breadth; our thoughts will also have the dimensions of thinking for data.

We attain these dimensions of data through our knowledge and experiences.

Every individual's knowledge and experiences will be unique and so are everyone's dimensions of thoughts.

We might be wondering how these dimensions of thought differs from person to person.

We might have gone to the same school and studied the same concepts listening to the lectures delivered by the same professors. But the way we analyze the data differs from person to person. Each one of them in the class will interpret and infer from the data as per his or her own thought process.

If we observe this with precision, whenever our mind receives some new data or information that is unknown to us, apart from storing the information in the mind to be recollected at later point of time whenever required, our mind will also analyze the stored data relevant for the received data and interprets it based on our past knowledge.

This aspect of analysis, interpretation, decision making and execution of the future actions based on these inferences differ from person to person that is unique to a person.

We call this as life or life stories or biography. Every person's life is unique.

There might be some situations and scenarios that are similar and have that matching and connectivity somewhere, but overall put together each person's life and experiences remain unique and so are the thoughts which reflect the uniqueness in thinking and unique thought process of a person.

What causes these Uniqueness of Thoughts and differences of interpretation of thoughts and thought process?

Can we say that the Dimensionality of thoughts create this Uniqueness of thoughts?

To make this easy to understand, take a simple scenario where the professor is teaching the students about how to Enjoy the Fruits of Life in a given joyful situation.

The levels of interpretation, analysis and inference taken by each of the students for this given statement differ based on their life experiences and dimensions of thought process.

As we have seen in Chapter 2, our thoughts flow through a series of stages throughout the Thought Management Lifecycle.

In this context, when the students hear the statement given by the professor 'Enjoying the fruits of Life', this unorganized data initiates the thought in a person through the external stimulation. This is the stage of Thought Occurrence.

Students who have heard of this before and students who have not heard of this before, both the groups perceive this information, scientifically termed as extra sensory perception or external stimulation that in turn stimulates the neurons and generates electrical impulses in our brain.

Next comes the stage of Thought Sustenance. In this scenario, students who have heard of this earlier already, ignore this statement.

Also people who don't feel any relevance for this statement tend to ignore this. So, the thought will not sustain longer and they tend to forget it and the Thought enters the final stage of the Thought Process: Thought Lapse.

This thought will be forgotten or lapses in the mind and again goes back to the initiation of the Thought Management Life Cycle: Thought Occurrence with new set of information or Thoughts.

But, if some students have never heard of this statement before and feel this statement to be relevant and applicable, tend to recognize that this is of some importance and relevance for them somewhere in their life. This is the stage of Thought Realization.

So their Thoughts have passed through the stages of Thought Occurrence, Thought Sustenance and Thought Realization.

Next stage is Thought Organization and Design.

Students in the class who feel the statement given by the professor 'Enjoying the fruits of life' to be applicable and relevant will try for organizing and designing their thoughts applicable for them in such a way that they start analyzing and interpreting the meaning in it and organize their thoughts to believe the truth or fact in it.

That is they design their belief system to accept the statement supporting with all their past experiences, knowledge and existing beliefs. This organization and design of thoughts is not so easy as it sounds and requires a lot of mental effort. It requires us to convince our mind and recollect our thoughts and then group our thoughts that support the statement and then organize and design our thoughts and Thought Process in such a way that we convince our belief system to accept this as a fact that is relevant and applicable for them.

All this thought process occurs in each one of us unknowingly and unconsciously without our knowledge and intervention. That's why brain is considered as one of the complex organs of human body and mind is considered as one of the miracles of the universe.

So, the thoughts that have passed through this stage of Thought Organization and Design will move to the next stage Thought Execution.

Thoughts which have not entered this stage will not be executed and worked upon by us and we tend to ignore that data or information that means we couldn't convince our belief system about the information we heard or received as reliable and valid.

We tend to ignore these things and it enters the final stage of Thought Lapse and the Thought Process Life Cycle ends for that particular thought and starts with a new thought with Thought Occurrence.

Next stage is the Thought Execution. This is the stage where we proceed with working on the idea or thought or start executing the thought. This is when new discoveries and inventions are made.

This is the stage where we take a decision to execute on the thoughts.

All the creative and innovative ideas take the shape into Reality.

Prototypes and Designs emerge as a result out of this stage initially. That means we convinced our mind belief system about our Thought Design to move to the next stage of Thought Execution.

We gather all the related data and information relevant for our Thought Design to start working on it and getting some shape to it and bringing it to Reality.

This stage involves both physical and mental work to materialize thoughts into Reality and work on it.

After Thought Execution stage comes the stage of Thought Outcome.

This is ideally considered the last stage of the Thought implementation and Manifestation that gets materialized into Reality that we can look and feel. This is the stage where Thought Outcome is finalized. We get to see the result of the Thought Execution stage.

Thought Execution stage will have the prototypes built and Thought Outcome is the final result or outcome of the built-in prototype.

To come to this stage, our thoughts need to pass through all the previous stages for which both physical and mental efforts are involved and convincing our belief system to proceed further with the Thought implementation and Execution that results in the Thought Outcome.

Any thought that passes this stage of Thought Execution that resulted in Thought Outcome will no longer remain a Thought. Because the thought has already taken the shape of an object that got already materialized.

Coming to the example of the statement we have considered in this scenario “Enjoying the fruits of Life”; once we have convinced our belief system of the mind to accept this statement and work towards implementing and working on it, our mind will start executing the thoughts supporting our belief system.

This is the most critical stage of Thought Process that decides the direction of our life.

During Thought Execution stage, we need to execute the thoughts organized and designed. The way we interpret these thoughts makes a lot of difference.

Some minds analyze this as ‘Enjoying’ as the execution stage of the Thought because the statement said ‘Enjoying the fruits of life’ and enjoyment is the execution part of it.

But some minds think in a different direction as to how can we enjoy the fruits of life?

What should we do to enjoy the fruits of life?

How are the most successful people living their lives?

What are the things they implemented to enjoy the fruits of life?

What do we need to work on in order to enjoy the fruits of life? And so on.....

That means some people think on the analytical aspects of the designed thoughts and establish their own way to execute their thoughts.

During this, some people tend to just follow others and some people have their own ways to execute their thoughts.

People who don’t analyze their thoughts just understand the statement as enjoying life and focus towards enjoyment in their lives without working towards anything and they convince their belief system that the goal of life is enjoyment.

We see this kind of behavior and thinking among youngsters and people below 18-20 yrs of age group specifically. I conducted a short survey and came up with my own questionnaire to understand the psychology and thought process of these people and the results showed that more than 60% of the group think alike towards this given statement but remaining 40% of people differ in their thoughts and opinions.

This thought process is what I feel distinguishes us and differentiates us from the rest of the group we are living with.

This is all dependent on the way we design and execute our thoughts that will result in the Thought Outcome materialized into a real time object or activity.

Our knowledge and past experiences will influence this stage of Thought Design and Thought Execution.

Dimensionality of Thoughts or Dimensional Thinking practices will form the key factors for analyzing and executing the thoughts during these stages.

Thought Management is a very vast subject that can be analyzed and understood in multiple directions and dimensions that specify its importance on an individual's life.

We live by our Thoughts and we lead our lives by our Thoughts which implies we are made by our Thoughts.

Thoughts define us and our lives and mastering the art of Thought Management and adapting to Uniqueness of Thoughts will help us master ourselves and our lives.

Dimensional Thinking is the one aspect that is gaining Prominence in the professional environment especially in the Corporate World.

Because individuals holding senior positions at senior levels of management and leadership are required to think in multiple dimensions and should have the mindset with dimensional thinking capabilities.

Being in the senior position of a manager or leader, requires us to think in several directions to analyze a particular situation or to assess the impact of some decision being taken or to take a crucial decision that decides the business criticality and market statistics of the business thus influencing the overall revenue and business growth rate in the market.

As a manager, you will be required to manage a group of managers and projects or a group of teams.

When it comes to managing a team or a group of teams, you should be able to manage every person in the team as each person will have a unique role to play. To manage so many teams and groups of people with different cultural backgrounds, different languages and locations and to convince them in making them understand the requirements is not a simple task.

This requires a lot of mental stability and maturity and the capability to convince the people about what you think and conveying the message to the right set of people at the right time in a way that they perceive the message or interpret the message in the right way as conveyed.

Project management involves business management and knowledge, interacting with various stakeholders of the business in order to understand the needs and requirements of the business and to get things done.

For this managers need to think from the directions of so many people involved in order to establish the synchronicity with them and understand them.

Dimensional Thinking plays an important role wherein one needs to think across several dimensions of thoughts for analyzing a problem or providing a solution to the problem. When given raw data or information, they need to analyze it thinking from the dimensional statistics of the data as to what is the reliability and genuineness of the data, how much the data and information received is valid, what is the volume of the data, what is the extension limitations of the information, across multiple systems and geographies.

To execute any project, understanding these concepts is essential to come up with the solution and execution strategies of the requirement.

Once they understand this, managers and leaders need to make people and the teams working with them understand this. For this, they need to reach to the mind levels of each person in the team to match with their frequency of mindset and thoughts. As seen earlier, each of them will have different dimensions of thoughts based on their past life and experiences.

They need to manage teams across geographies which require them to understand their thoughts, work culture and environment and all the remaining aspects in order to have the control on the teams.

Managing and leading diversified teams across locations requires the leaders to think unique and different from others so as to have the control of the situation and the work to get things done.

(Leadership is entirely a different subject and we will not be covering on leadership practices in this book).

We will only focus on the importance of dimensional thinking and analysis for leaders to manage teams and organizations.

Leaders need to implement and follow unique thought management practices and strategies. Thought Design, Thought Execution and Thought Outcome are the most important stages to be focused upon, that will result in the outcome as expected or will decide the outcome of a thought. Leaders are required to be creative and innovative in their thoughts. They should have the ability to take the most critical decisions at times that will decide the reputation of the organization or will have impact on the revenue or growth rate of the business. So, leaders are required to adapt to the dimensional thinking mindset before they take any decision or execute any activity in their role.

If we notice, not all leaders' execution and management strategies are similar. They remain unique for them to have their uniqueness and unique identity as a leader.

This is possible because they must have already programmed their mind to think unique and their Thought Process Life Cycle was different.

This doesn't mean the Thought Lifecycle was different for them. This means, after Thought Occurrence, Thought Sustenance and Thought Realization, their Thought Organization and Design and Thought Execution was different that had resulted in the Unique Thought Outcome which has materialized into Reality fetching them the results they expected or making their dreams, wishes and desires a Reality.

We have already seen what attributes define these stages in the Thought Process for a person that make the person unique and have his own identity amongst others.

Dimensional Thinking is a very broad concept of Thought Management. As we grow with time and experience, the mind will adapt to the dimensions more; that is we start thinking and analyzing people and things around us with more depth and interpretation. This defines the dimensions of Thoughts.

That's why we say some people are broad-minded and some people are narrow minded. Some people are extroverts and some people are introverts in thinking.

Their dimensions of Thought Process will define what kind of person they are and creates their identity and recognition.

Dimensional Thought Process is the ability to think with dimensions of data across all the stages of the Thought Process. This is nowadays being widely accepted in the Corporate World because of its unique characteristics achieved through unique ways of Thinking through Unique Thought Process.

8

Where is the Concept of Thought Management and Unique Thinking applicable

Thought Management is a discipline. It is the way of Organized Thinking which paves a path for direction in life.

Uniqueness in Thinking and Unique Thought Process will define the identity and recognition of a person.

Next question that comes up is where can we exactly apply these Thought Management and Uniqueness in Thinking Practices.

As we already came across many scenarios where we implemented these concepts of Thought Management and Uniqueness in Thinking practices in the previous chapters, how can we apply these concepts in personal and professional life.

(We will see about how we can implement unique thinking practices in day to day life in detail in the next chapter).

Unique Thinking forms the fundamental aspect of recognition of a person because **we are what we Think and Act. Our thoughts define our actions.**

We are made of thoughts that we act upon for any given situation or context. But how we react to situations and handle various situations and scenarios and manage various groups of people are defined by our thoughts and thought process. Even if Thought Process and Thought Lifecycle Management remain the same for all of us, the kind of thoughts that get generated in our mind during the Thought Process and Thought Lifecycle Management phases differ from person to person.

As we have seen, Thoughts are not gifted by birth. Our intelligence quotient IQ and the psychological creative abilities of the brain might be inherited from our parents and ancestors through our genetics, but programming our mind to adapt to the unique thinking mindset is always within our abilities and capabilities. All that we need to learn is to recognize our potential to do things or take up any tasks. Thought Management and Uniqueness in Thinking is applicable in all the aspects of life. There is no situation or scenario where we don't require thinking or acting. Whether we do it consciously or unconsciously from the day we are born we are thinking about several aspects of life and acting upon it.

As an infant, we had thought about several things unconsciously and acted upon them without our conscious knowledge.

Because a child knows to cry if there is any problem or something is occurring which he or she doesn't like.

That means the Thought that gets generated in their mind for that particular situation commands their mind to act upon communicating it through some source in the form of crying. We adults communicate it through our words and actions. But the maturity of the mind and the thoughts grow as the infants brain gets developed by age and surroundings and experiences.

From the time we wake up in the morning till the time we sleep; consciously or subconsciously we think about any task or activity and act upon it.

That means we are implementing the Thought Management process in our life without our knowledge.

When we think about our career and profession, we all want to be unique and stand out in the crowd that is we all want to have that recognition and identification for ourselves. This can be achieved through Unique Thinking Practices.

There is no such specific method to learn how to think unique. **Unique Thinking is not a standard subject to learn but a practice to develop and improve.**

Program your mind to think different from others. Our general tendency is to just follow others but we never tend to think towards thinking unique and adapting ourselves to a unique thinking mindset.

I have observed this generic mindset among many people; the reason being we can't think so much or we don't have the capability of thinking so much. But I say this statement is wrong. When you think this way, you are subconsciously programming your mind to adapt to a negative state of thought.

Our mind at times cannot differentiate between a positive thought and a negative thought and starts executing this thought in the Thought Process.

In order to make our mind to understand the difference between a positive thought and a negative thought, we need to input our mind with the required data for it to understand and realize the exact differences between positivity and negativity and to determine which path to choose. As I mentioned earlier, mind is considered to be one of the miracles of universe and our physical brain the most complex organ of human body.

It all depends on how we program our mind. Our mind is like the loyal servant gifted to us by birth. It listens to whatever we say and executes whatever we command.

We need to input the right set of information for it to work on our wishes and dreams.

That is we need to have control on our mind and thoughts.

Like how we don't leave children to wander anywhere and eat anything, we should also not let our mind wander anywhere and input any data. That is we need to have that control on our mind and set some direction for our thoughts.

You might be asking that to have control and command on the mind and setting a direction for the thought process is fine but what sets up this direction for the thought process?

Is it not a Thought?

For this, the answer is Yes. That is also a Thought.

It is a thought that gets triggered in our mind based on our past experiences and knowledge, likes and dislikes, dreams and desires and sets up a direction for the Thought Process as to what we need to think and what we need to act upon.

You must have heard about this most popular statements.

We are the creators of our own Destiny.

We are the Masters of our Mind.

This means our mind has the unique characteristic of self-controlling and self-programming.

Then why do we need to control it and program it explicitly?

We all keep talking about mind and hear people talk about mind and mindfulness, but what is mind and where is it?

Can we see our mind? Is the mind visible? Is it a physical object? Is mind an organ in our human body?

Has anyone of us ever tried to analyze this and understand this about mind?

Most of us must not have tried thinking in these aspects.

Brain is a physical organ in the human body but the mind is not. Then what is mind? Where can we find mind?

How mind can program itself and control itself but then again we are required to program it?

This sounds miraculous and a concept completely unknown to us. We never bother to analyze on these aspects because we can't think so much. The answer is simple.

Mind is the invisible organ of the biological body while brain is the visible organ. If we talk in scientific terms, brain is made of nerve cells or neurons which generate electrical impulses or signals that trigger the thoughts in our mind.

Our brain is a neural network or a collection of neural networks. It has got countless number of neurons interconnected with each other that forms the neural linkage of networks. These neurons communicate with each other through electrical impulses. The output of the neuron is also an electrical signal. This interconnectivity or linkage between neural networks and the transfer of data or information is biologically controlled by certain chemical combinations and reactions within our body.

This forms the biological functioning of the human brain.

Then what forms the functioning of the mind? Thoughts

Thoughts are the inputs we give to our mind for performing and executing a task. We input our mind with our thoughts to get the required thought outcome.

Where do these thoughts come from?

Thoughts come from our past experiences and life and information stored in our mind and through external stimulation.

Unique Thinking describes how we can input our thoughts with what kind of information in order to get the desired thought outcome that materializes and manifests into Reality.

We have various meditation and thought management practices that teach us how to improve our mind power and help in materializing and manifesting our thoughts.

(We will cover some of these methods in the next chapters).

We all know the importance of Meditation and Yoga in day to day life. There are many art of living organizations that have already come up to bring this awareness among people which forms the essential part of everyday life.

Why do we need to Meditate?

Meditation helps our mind reach to the levels of universal oneness of mind.

Whenever we meditate, our mind will be cleared from unnecessary and unwanted thoughts through which we can achieve the calmness of mind and clarity of mind.

When our mind becomes calm, it tends to absorb and retrieve more data from the universal library (we already saw this concept of universal library in chapter 3) and utilize this information for achieving the results it wanted or to get things done.

That's why the most creative and innovative thoughts are generated when we are calm and relaxed.

A clumsy and a distracting mind will only create more disturbance and confusion. This means it is not in a state to receive the required information though it is available with it and around it.

So, we apply these concepts of thought management in almost every activity we perform and every task we do.

But what matters is how we apply this thought management and concepts of uniqueness of thoughts in thinking different from others.

We apply these principles of thought management in almost everything unknowingly because our life is made up of thoughts and activities that we perform.

From the time we start our day till we end our day, we tend to work on something or think about something; without doing these activities nobody's life exists. When we think about something which is known to us that means we are recollecting the data and tasks that we performed or the words we spoke; what we spoke; with whom we spoke or what we did and why we did and the cause and effect of it.

That is we are recollecting and memorizing the data but not analyzing anything new. Even if we are analyzing what we already know and what we have already come across; it is like memorizing the information or recollecting our stored thoughts in the brain. There is nothing new here that we are working on or nothing creative and innovative we are doing here. This can be considered as one of the examples for Thought Reoccurrence.

In these kind of situations, we focus more on the Thought Occurrence, Thought Sustenance, Thought Realization stages of Thought Process followed by Thought Reoccurrences, Thought Continuity and Thought Lapse.

Thought Organization and Design, Thought Execution and Thought Outcome stages are also applicable, but they have very minimal role to play as we are not directing our thoughts towards Thought Execution for generating a new outcome. There are not much creative and analytical capabilities involved in this.

So, this thought process occurs smoothly sometimes without our knowledge because we don't put in much efforts to recollect something we already know.

There is also nothing here ideally to think unique about until and unless we want to have a unique perception and analysis for things which had already happened. These kinds of situations we come across when it comes to relationships where we want to memorize or recollect things or incidents which had already happened and have our unique perception towards it.

In these kind of scenarios, we can say that Thought Management and Unique Thought Process play a crucial role in deciding our relationships with others.

Same scenario can be applicable for the couples and the love relationships where people tend to continuously memorize and recollect the past incidents, situations, conversations, etc.

That is they are continuously programming their mind to analyze on the things already happened. Some people also adapt to unique thinking in such scenarios as to how they can improve it in the future.

So, more focus on the recollections and memories and adapting to unique thought process about their already existing analysis or perception and ways to improve it in the future.

With this, thinking with a positive or negative mind will decide the status of the relationships.

People who direct their thinking towards positive thought process tend to continue their relationships while people who direct their thinking towards negative thought process tend to break or cause damage for their relationships.

Their uniqueness in Thinking will be the **thought factor** for deciding their status of relationships depending on their experiences with each other in a relationship.

So, Thought Management and Unique Thought Process are applicable for family, love life and relationships also. We have already seen how it is applicable for our career and professional life.

The more we understand the applicability of thoughts in our life the more we come to know about their importance in our life and the role unique thinking plays in our life for creating our uniqueness quotient and unique identity among others.

Unique Thinking is not a standard methodology or a principle to follow but a continuous practice of enlightenment and improvement to execute and implement.

If we recognize and understand the applicability of thoughts in our life, we realize that thoughts form the essence and source of living for each one of us and there is no situation or a scenario where we don't need to think or act. Thoughts and actions form our day to day aspects of life. This is common for all of us; but what makes us different from others is how we design and define our thoughts and actions in our day to day life that make us think unique and act unique.

9

Unique Thinking for day to day life and how to improve our Thinking capabilities

Uniqueness of Thoughts is applicable in everyday life. We all are made up of thoughts and how we manage these thoughts will form the most crucial aspect of thought management.

Thought management is a discipline. It is an art of designing and managing our life. Once we are able to manage our thoughts, we will be able to manage our life and have control on our life.

We will be able to design our life the way we like and the way we want it to be.

We can apply these principles of uniqueness in thinking and practice in everyday life.

It is not a standard methodology or practice that can be studied and forgotten or a principle which can be used during certain critical scenarios and situations. It is an art of leading life by designing our thoughts to get the results we want.

Uniqueness and Management of Thoughts is the subject that is becoming popular in this digital era of transformation where it is critical for each of us to deal with our thoughts and program our mind to achieve the results we want.

Thought Management is a discipline that is applicable in almost all the phases of life. There is no gender or age bifurcation for adapting to these principles and practices because of its relevance and applicability in every step of life.

From the time we wake up in the morning and start off the day, we program our mind to execute things for us. We start our day with meditation or yoga or a walk outside or with a light music that peps our morning mood which is very crucial for the rest of the day.

Either this morning routine activity is pre-programmed if we are used to follow this or we newly program it to the mind to follow this if we have not followed it earlier. No matter what the situation is, we need to tell our mind to do something for us or to allow us to perform the activities we want to do. If we don't say it to the mind, it will not understand what to do next.

All this process happens automatically in the mind without our conscious intervention and knowledge and sometimes we are not aware of the activities and thoughts circulating within us.

This means our mind executes things at the micro and nano levels of speed and with precision that we don't realize the occurrence of it within us.

Our human body's mechanism is designed in such a way which means our mind and body are already preprogrammed to carry out human biological functions even before we are born.

Each and every activity that happens within us is a thought pre programmed to perform some action. This is how we humans are designed. We tend to perceive things and manage our thoughts but we don't have the control on the already programmed biological cycle and thought process. It is self sustained and self controlled.

We can just improve our quality of thoughts through our knowledge and wisdom.

Leaving behind the concept of thoughts responsible for the functioning of the biological process for human existence that is not under our control to manage, we can choose our thoughts to input our mind in day to day life.

What we input in our mind will result in the output of our mind that we can see and observe in the form of speech or actions.

Our day to day life requires us to be busy with work all day long and all through this process we deal with our mind unconsciously and subconsciously for getting our activities and work done. This is a repetitive process that occurs in us everyday.

When we are required to perform some tasks or come up with some creative and innovative activities as part of our job, we require our mind to come up with some thoughts to complete that task. In such scenarios, the data and information we had input to our mind and the knowledge we possess will be applicable in providing required input for our mind and to proceed with thought process and again the thoughts pass through the stages of the Thought lifecycle for getting the results we want.

We can improve our thinking capabilities through reading good books, informative articles and journals, meeting good people from our colleagues and friends and from our family.

Meditation and Mind Control exercises also help in programming our mind and designing our thoughts to a certain extent. It provides the direction to our thoughts by taking the help from the universal mind for retrieving the required and relevant data.

We already know that our mind is a search engine for querying and retrieving the data we want. We need to program it for fetching us the results in a way that we want.

We need the help of our mind in almost every activity we do. When we talk to people, we think about what to talk how to talk and what not to talk. Samething applies for friends and family also. We have our own ways of conversations and maintaining relationships. We will have our own ways of handling different people and different relationships within our family itself.

Our ways of conversing and behaving with our mother will be different, the way we converse and behave with our father will be different, the way we maintain our relationships with our brothers, sisters and spouse will be different. Likewise the way we behave with our friends will be different.

Who has programmed our mind to differentiate these people and relationships with these people?

When we are behaving and conversing with people in different ways it implies our mind knows the differences of relationships with these people. That means our mind has this data already with it input through external stimulation.

During any strained relationship or disturbances in relationship we think of ways to improve it or rectify it. We think about what is the problem and try to find a solution for the problem which forms the outcome of our thought process.

This is also applicable for the relationships between married couples and people in love. Most of the psychiatrists and psychology consultants use these thought management practices and methods in analyzing the issues and providing a resolution for the issues.

They provide counselling for changing and improving the thought process and adapt to thought management effectively.

Same thing is applicable for the career and issues related to professional life.

Our everyday work life requires us to deal with different groups of people coming from different locations and speaking different languages from multicultural and multi-lingual backgrounds. We need to manage different teams and handle several challenging tasks and come across several challenging situations. All this will require us to program our mind in a way capable enough to handle these kind of situations.

This requires efficient thought management and unique thinking methods and practices.

We can take the examples of some scenarios where unique thinking can be applied for maintaining healthy relationships between our friends and family.

Relationships are given a lot of significance nowadays with almost everyone we come across; friends, colleagues and families in particular. Also having healthy relationships between peers and seniors and with the team in the professional environment has become more important for creating and maintaining an integrated and productive work culture for establishing team spirit, team integrity and improving work performance.

Communication and Collaboration within the team and across teams is being recognized as one of the most important parameters for team performance and productivity within defined timelines.

We all know that effective communication and collaboration is not possible without maintaining good rapport and relationships with the people around.

Managing different groups of individuals and different teams and establishing good relationships requires different ways of distinguished thinking and unique thinking aspects.

We are required to think from their direction of thoughts to understand their perceptions and perspectives of analyzing and executing things.

To manage so many people with such varied backgrounds and cultures with various directions of thinking is not as simple as it sounds and being a manager and a leader you will be required to deal with every individual in the team and handle all sorts of issues arising out of any unexpected or unavoidable situations.

We have seen that dimensional thinking helps us analyze the situation in every direction possible by thinking about it from the volume, length, breadth aspects of the data and other analytical and dimensional parameters of the problem or the situation for coming up with the appropriate solution relevant for the particular context.

When it comes to dealing with personal relationships with friends and family our thought process altogether takes a different perspective and direction.

In personal relationships, our thoughts are more directed towards psychological and emotional factors rather than monitoring, directing and controlling factors unlike our relationships maintained at professional environment.

At professional work place, we think on the grounds of decision making, problem solving, managing, directing and controlling parameters.

That means our direction of thinking is more inclined towards being productive and thoughtful taking accountability of handling psychological and emotional factors involved.

While in personal relationships, our direction of thinking is focused more towards sensitive, emotional and psychological factors that would involve the internal characteristics and inbuilt thoughts of an individual on a sensitive and a personal level.

For example, when it comes to personal relationships, we will be required to take care of our parents, in-laws, spouse, children, friends and other family relations within and outside family.

We will be required to understand and interact with people of different ages; convincing them and understanding them requires some directions to our thoughts and our thought process.

How do we handle situations at personal level by ways of unique thinking?

As we have seen unique thinking is not a principle or a methodology but rather a practice that can be followed in every phase and every aspect of our life.

We know how important our personal relationships are for us and so we need to understand and realize the importance of thinking unique in order to be recognized at an individual and personal level among our friends and family.

We all know that managing with disturbances and issues in personal relationships is as critical as managing with issues at workplace. We need

to understand the balance and the equilibrium that we have to maintain between personal life and professional life.

Personal growth is equally important for growth in career. This is the reason why relationships consultation and psychology consultation is gaining prominence in the healthcare sector with the increase in the necessity for solving issues at personal level.

If our personal relationships are healthy, our professional career will be successful and this is a well known fact clearly evident from the life experiences and biographies of some of the most successful people.

So, how can we think unique that can help in improving our relationships at personal level (we have already seen how can we adapt to unique thinking practices at professional level).

There are various types of relationships that we need to handle as a person. It's very common for all of us to have issues starting from micro level to the issues having considerable impact with the relationships we come across during some situation or context at some point of time.

Managing issues with parents will be different from managing issues with spouse and children. When it comes to managing issues with elders and families our thoughts travel through the phase of Thought Reoccurrence where we tend to remember and recollect things from our adolescence and childhood and accordingly manage and handle things at sensitive and emotional levels.

So, in this scenario all thoughts travel through the phases of

Thought Reoccurrence – Thought Sustenance – Thought Realization – Thought Execution- Thought Outcome

Thought Continuity is followed until the issue gets resolved or expected outcome is achieved followed by Thought Lapse.

Again a new thought generates with the occurrence of thought during the phase of Thought Occurrence.

This process will remain similar for the relationships with Spouse and Children as well when our direction of thinking is focused on Thought Reoccurrence and Thought Continuity until we reach to the state of expected Thought Outcome.

Along with our professional life, our personal life also requires us to deal with difficult and challenging situations at times.

We are also at times required to think creative and innovative while handling personal relationships. So our creative and innovative Thinking comes into picture here, where our thoughts travel through the phases of Thought Execution until it reaches Thought Outcome.

Unique Thinking and Positive mindset will help in maintaining good relationships and deal with issues at personal and emotional levels.

For handling these kind of issues, our mind needs to analyze and understand the data relevant for the situation, process the data and provide the result with the existing information and knowledge based on our past experiences and situations we had come across in our life.

If we face a situation where we are required to deal with unknown problems which we have never come across, then we need to input the required data for our mind for processing and analyzing the situation and providing the required solution.

For this again, our mind needs to go through the phases of Thought Process and Thought Lifecycle where it fetches and retrieves the data from the visible environment, situations and people surrounding us through external stimulation or retrieve the required information and knowledge from the universal library by connecting with the abundantly available pool of data and knowledge around us.

So, we need to program our mind in such a way to understand the relationships, various forms of relationships, how to deal with issues in relationships and to provide solutions for the issues coming with relationships.

This way we can adapt to different ways of thinking because our thoughts and thought process differ from individual to individual even though the situation and context remain similar.

Uniqueness of Thoughts in such situations will define our distinguishing identity as an individual at a personal level.

Each of us have different ways of identity with people and solving problems. That means we are unknowingly adapting to a distinguished and a unique way of thinking and following a unique thought process for providing solutions for these problems.

When it comes to managing and maintaining relationships at personal level, psychological, emotional and sentimental factors are given more priority. Some of us also believe in fortune, luck and karma when dealing with most important aspects and people in our life.

I personally had gone through various situations in my life that forced me to think on the aspects of fortune, luck and karma keeping apart logical reasoning of the situations and thinking on the managing and directing levels for getting things done.

But I gradually realized that we can fine tune this thought process by way of changing and directing our thoughts to focus on the aspects of thinking different and unique.

When we come across a challenging and a difficult phase in life, our mind will be forced to think according to our environment, surroundings and the people surrounding us.

During this time, if we develop the capability within us to control our mind and take it to the state of calmness for analyzing the things happening with the state of thoughtfulness for taking a decision or coming up with a solution, we can achieve wonders in our life. But to achieve this level of mind, we need to have complete control and command on our mind for it to behave and act as we expect during these kinds of difficult and challenging times.

Adapting to unique thinking methods and practices and implementing them regularly will help us to reach to this state of unique thinking mindset during challenging times where our mind reaches to the state of mindfulness and thoughtfulness for handling situations and to deal with people we come across.

This uniqueness of thoughts and the capability of being able to reach to the state of thoughtfulness for attaining the unique thinking mindset and follow unique thought process will make us standout distinguished, positive and different from others that will create the unique identity for us.

How to improve our thinking capabilities?

Thought Management is a repetitive and a recurring process throughout our life. It is a continuous thought lifecycle process that is to be programmed and managed as per our needs and demands.

For this we need to continuously improve our thinking patterns and methodologies to keep

ourselves and our thought process up to date with the day to day changes and needs in life.

Some of the practices that we can follow for attaining unique thinking mindset are mentioned below:

- **Input of quality data into mind.**

We are what we think. What we input in our mind will form the Output of our mind. The quality of input data forms one of the most critical components for processing of our thoughts because the Thought Process lifecycle for that particular thought is processed based on the input data that will subsequently result in the Thought Execution and Thought Outcome.

- **Interacting with appropriate group of people.**

The group of people we interact with will have considerable impact on our thoughts.

People with Positive mindset will reflect positive energy and vibrations while people with negative mindset will reflect negative vibrations and thoughts.

These people usually tend to input others' minds with the same data and influence the people surrounding them.

Positive minded people will have positive influence on their surroundings and people surrounding them while negative minded people will have negative influence on the environment and the people around them.

At times we will be required to be Assertive during our discussions and conversations.

Assertive Thinking is being widely recognized in the professional environment nowadays for getting the fruitful outcome out of discussions and conversations.

❖ **Improving the power of our mind through regular meditation practices.**

Regular practice of meditation and mind control to reach to the state of calmness for attaining the states of Thoughtfulness and Thoughtlessness will help in improving the power of our mind.

We already know that the state of Thoughtlessness is the highest states of mind one can achieve where our mind reaches to the state of having NO THOUGHTS.

We should not misunderstand this with the state of Mindlessness or distracted and confused state of mind.

We can attain this state of Thoughtlessness only through regular and dedicated Meditation and Mind Control practices.

When we reach to this state of Thoughtlessness, our mind will attain the capability to connect with the oneness of mind and oneness of universe and to retrieve the information from the universal library; we know that our mind is the search engine for querying the required results from the universal library.

Practicing regular meditation for attaining the mental capability of reaching to the state of Thoughtlessness will form the path for improving and attaining power of mind and subsequently help in manifesting and materializing the thoughts into Reality that we can see.

❖ Listening to inspiring and Motivational Talks

- When we listen to the motivational talks and biographies of the successful people, we are inputting our mind with the qualitative data that gets further analyzed and processed in our mind which will result in getting the required Thought Outcome.
- Like how good food and nutrition is essential for the healthy body, good food for thought is essential for the healthy mind.
- We know that we are made up of thoughts and the quality of our thoughts differentiate us from others that will form the distinguishing criteria for our thought process which forms our unique identity and uniqueness quotient.

❖ Reading the biographies of successful people and learning from it

Reading and listening are the ways in which we give our mind the Food for Thought.

For some of us, Reading is like a meditation practice where our mind reaches to the state of relaxation and calmness for analyzing and understanding the data and information and process it.

Reading the biographies of successful people will help us in learning from their life and experiences that forms the reference data for our thoughts for analyzing and processing the events and activities in our life.

Reading and understanding the experiences that has lead to the success of others is like feeding our mind with good thoughts and having good food for thought forms the essential nutrition for the healthy mind and to attain the state of mindfulness and Thoughtfulness.

❖ **Allowing our mind to interact with the universal mind to achieve the capability of retrieving the abundantly available data**

We already know that what we input to our mind will form the output of our mind. So it's very important to provide nutrition to our mind by way of inputting right set of quality data.

This will help our mind become more energetic and attain the capability of thinking more positive.

Like how our body needs nutrition, our mind also needs nutrition to be healthy and positive.

We provide nutrition to our body through intake of food but how do we provide nutrition to our mind?

We can provide nutrition to our mind through Dhyana or Silence and relaxation by reaching to the state of Calmness and Thoughtlessness.

We need to program our mind to recollect the positive memories and incidents that had happened in the past. Recollection of negative incidents will only result in negative outcome.

When we reach to the state of Thoughtlessness or the state of having NO THOUGHTS that means we have achieved the highest form of Meditation in which our mind interacts with the oneness of mind and oneness of universe. This is when we experience SILENCE during meditation.

This is the next level of Mindful Breathing or Breath Awareness Meditation and Affirmative Meditation in which we are required to reach to the state of calmness of mind through chanting some powerful words and syllables called Mantras that will have impact on our mind OR Positive Affirmations to program our mind to think positive and retrieve the required information from the universal library for achieving the required results we wish for.

Next to these mind levels is the level of mind to reach to the state of Thoughtlessness in which we experience and listen to SILENCE; some people also can feel and hear the vibrations of the universe in this state.

Practicing meditation regularly and nourishing our mind with positive thoughts can make wonders and create miracles in getting the results we want.

❖ Understanding the concepts and relevance of the oneness of mind.

We need to basically understand the concepts of oneness of mind to implement mindfulness and thoughtfulness in our life.

Realizing the importance and relevance of the power of mind and oneness of mind is essential for the success in life and also to create that unique recognition and identity for the self as well as for others.

The THOUGHT that occurs at the right moment by way of Mindfulness and Thoughtfulness that will have a distinguishing impact either on our own self or on others will signify the relevance of our mind power with the oneness of mind.

❖ Meeting spiritual and knowledgeable people and understanding things from their life and experiences.

By speaking to intellectual and spiritual people, we get to learn from their life and experiences.

Every person who is successful today must have crossed several hurdles and obstacles and must have gone through several positive and negative experiences in his or her life.

Everyone of us will have our unique set of positive and negative experiences.

By listening and understanding of other's success stories and biographies we get to realize about ourselves in a better way and recognize our potential of getting what we want in life.

From my personal experiences, I can say that whenever we meet intellectually spiritual and knowledgeable people, their positive vibrations and positivity of mind will have a recognizable impact on our ways of thinking and Thought Process. **But we need to realize this to implement this for achieving the success that we desire.**

❖ Adapting to a healthy lifestyle and healthy mindset through positive thinking practices.

We need to practice thinking about positive things, positive minded people, positive scenarios and situations that we had come across in life. When we think about positive and good things that make us emotionally and psychologically satisfied and happy, unconsciously and unknowingly we get to adapt to a healthy mindset that will result in a healthy lifestyle.

Continuously programming our mind with positive thoughts and positive affirmations will not only influence our visible mind but will also influence our invisible mind for connecting with the oneness of mind.

Meditation through positive affirmations is one of the best ways to achieve a positive thinking mindset.

❖ **Realizing the importance of positivity and positive thinking in our life**

In order to adapt to a positive lifestyle, we need to first realize the importance of positivity and positive thinking in our life. It's very common for everyone of us to come across positive and negative situations and meet with positive and negative minded people.

People with positive mindset will reflect positivity in their attitude while people with negative mindset will have negative attitude and negative ways of doing things. They tend to influence others also the same way.

In such situations, to attain our positive state of mind, we need to completely understand and realize the importance of living by positivity and adapting to positive ways of thinking.

Speaking with intellectually spiritual and successful people will help us understand and realize the importance of adapting to positive thinking practices and following a positive way of life.

❖ Realizing and understanding the importance of designing and organizing our thoughts for executing them to get the required outcome.

Designing and organizing our thoughts is very crucial for getting the outcome we want. If the thoughts are not organized and designed properly, the same will pass through the phases of Thought Execution that will result in Thought Outcome.

So, before the thought passes through the phase of Thought Execution, it has to be properly designed and organized.(We have seen in detail in chapter3 about the process and significance of Organized Thinking).

Organized Thinking is all about how we can sequentially organize or prioritize or execute the elements of a Thought in a structure or hierarchy of Thought Process.

Proper designing and organizing of thoughts is the crucial factor for deciding the quality outcome. Inputting our mind with appropriate data and retrieving the required set of data form the most important criteria for deciding the Thought Outcome.

- Memorizing the positive incidents, we have come across in our life and remembering the positive minded people we had come across.

Positive mindset will have a positive impact on a person's life. To achieve positive state of mind, we need to continuously program our mind with positive set of thoughts. This can be achieved through memorizing and recollecting positive incidents and remembering positive minded people we had come across in life.

People with positive mindset will reflect positivity whereas people with negative mindset will reflect negative vibrations. We need to make sure of ourselves that we realize and follow positivity of mind and live positive way of life.

- **Attaining the state of clarity of mind and calmness of mind through mind control and improvement techniques**

To achieve clarity of our thoughts and mind, we need to reach to the levels of calmness of mind and the state of Thoughtlessness where we get to completely know about ourselves and realize about ourselves in the state of calmness at the higher levels of mind.

To reach to these states of mind, we need to program our mind and develop that control on our mind to listen to our inputs and execute things as we want.

Breath awareness meditation, Affirmative Meditation, Thoughtfulness and Mindfulness meditation practices, input of right set of quality data, meeting intellectually spiritual and knowledgeable people, having control on our thoughts and our mind, watching good content that will help us achieve knowledge and improve the ways of thinking, adapt to the methods of analyzing things with precision for getting the clarity of thoughts, etc., will help to gain control over mind.

All these qualities and practices will lead in improving our Thinking capabilities and for achieving higher levels of thinking thus resulting in higher values of life.

We need to realize this:

We are what we think.

10

Concepts of Thought Management and Unique Thought Process with oneness of mind and oneness of universe for getting the results we want

By now, we understood that our mind is like the search engine that queries and retrieves the data from the universal library upon commanding and requesting it to fetch the required results.

But how is it possible for the mind to retrieve the information from the universal mind?

First of all, we need to know what this universal mind is.

Universal mind is nothing but the intelligence of the universe. We already know that we are surrounded by abundantly available knowledge and information. Universe is made up of energy that binds the particles together which gives it some tangible form that is visible to us.

We can't see the energy but we can only feel it. Likewise, we can't see invisible matter we can only feel it.

Human eye can perceive the wavelengths between 390 to 750 nanometers.

The maximum visual acuity of the human eye is 0.4 arc minutes. At 4 inches, the maximum human eye needs is 2190 ppi/dpi.

(ppi is the measure of pixel density in some direction).

Human eye (20/20) rated by Snellen eye chart statistical data, can see up to 300 micro radians of visual acuity and has a near point of 25 cm.

Likewise the maximum range of human hearing includes sound frequencies from about 15 to 18000 waves or cycles per second.

General range of hearing for young people is 20 Hz to 20 KHz.

However, there are animals who have better hearing than that of humans.

E.g.: Moth, Bat, Owl, Elephant, Dog, Cat, Horse, Dolphin, etc., have extraordinary hearing capabilities many times better than humans.

Dogs can hear upto 40 Hz to 60 KHz.

Cats can hear upto 45 KHz – 65 Khz.

Mice can hear upto 95 KHz.

(Human sensory perceptions content source: Wikipedia).

This means these animals are more intelligent than humans and have more knowledge because of their advanced sensory perceptions and capabilities.

So, we humans have some limitations for our biological functioning of the human body and we have to accept it and live with it.

As I already mentioned, mind is an invisible organ of the human body that connects with universal mind and intelligence.

Each of us is gifted with this miracle of mind; we call it as secondary mind or subconscious mind.

Our subconscious mind is our gateway for the universal intelligence. We need to have the capability to open the doors of our mind for accessing the data.

Subconscious mind is the invisible mind that interacts with the invisible universal mind while conscious mind is the invisible mind that interacts with the visible universal intelligence.

Conscious mind analyses and interprets the worldly data while subconscious mind analyzes and interprets the universal oneness of data.

We call it as oneness of mind and oneness of universe.

This means universal mind has the characteristic of oneness of existence i.e., it is a single entity spread across everywhere which is unique for every aspect of time and context and for every individual.

There are several research programs conducted for understanding this universal oneness of mind and this was proved to be correct. Many of us are not aware of this because we don't usually focus towards this subject and usually tend to ignore it. We human beings believe something visible and not believe in something invisible because our minds are programmed that way from childhood by our parents and elders to think practically and to believe in something which is only visible; not understanding the fact that our invisible mind is within us and working for us like a loyal servant for getting what we want.

We require both conscious mind and subconscious mind to interact with the materialistic world and the universal intelligence. Our conscious mind is like our self-awareness and knowledge that tells us what to believe, what not to believe, what to do, what not to do, what is right and what is wrong based on our experiences, awareness and knowledge of the worldly materialistic things and visible things. Our subconscious mind is the mind that interacts with universal oneness of mind for attaining the awareness and knowledge we require. This is a higher state of mind and higher level of mind which is already within us without we being aware of this.

That's why they say many of us are not aware of the potential hidden within us. This is the reason behind that; we have the infinite invisible treasure and knowledge bank hidden within us and we are not even aware of it and never bother to think about it or realize it.

That means we are consciously still not awakened to realize the unconscious potential within us. It is our choice to get it to Reality or not. People who have achieved the higher states of mind realize this and people who are with the lower levels of mind don't realize the hidden power and potential inside them.

Our unconscious oneness of mind interacts with the oneness of the universe. We can call it as oneness of mind and oneness of universe because there are no multiple minds that interact with multiple universes. There might be multiple universes beyond our solar system but when we say universe it is to be understood as the invisible energy and matter existing in space which we call it as oneness of universe.

Our unconscious or subconscious mind is the invisible mind that is within each of us. Some realize it but some don't realize it. There is an invisible mind that is spread across each of us. So, somewhere somehow everyone is connected through our mind knowingly or unknowingly. But it is not required for all of us to get the same data, be similar and behave similar or to know each other. It is not mandatory that we need to know one another if minds are connected. We will get to know about people depending on our situations and circumstances though we are unconsciously connected from before.

We only get to know people whom we talk to or we go around with or surrounding us. This is the process of a normal human existence and behavior. It is taken care by our conscious mind. It is like our self defense system that warns us and protects us from worldly problems.

The theory and concept of the working of the subconscious mind is very huge and entirely different area of research. So we will not be covering these topics in detail in this book but we will focus more towards certain aspects of oneness of mind with Thought Management and Unique Thought Process and how to get the results we want.

As we have already seen, our subconscious mind is like a loyal servant for us that gets us the information and the results we want. All that we need to do is constantly program it and make it understand about our exact requirements and that's all it will get it for us.

Many of us don't understand this concept of oneness of mind and don't believe that we have hidden treasure within us in the form of our mind. To realize the existence of the unconscious mind within us, one needs to reach to the higher levels of mind. Meditation and mastering of mind are some of the practices for attaining higher levels of consciousness. Only when we realize the existence of it, we can start working with it.

This needs a lot of self-discipline and self-control on us our body and mind. We need to understand what we are, who we are and what we want. Then only we can tell our mind what to do and what to get.

Without self-discipline and self-control, we can't reach to the higher levels of mind and unless we reach to this state of mind where we start feeling and realizing the oneness of the mind and oneness of the universe, we don't understand what to do with the abundantly available wealth and power within us in the form of our mind.

This requires a healthy lifestyle, healthy physical and mental inputs and food for thoughts, practices, regular meditation, spending some amount of time in nature and so on, like how yoga is the exercise of the physical body, meditation is the exercise of the mind but most of us don't recognize the importance of meditation. We only bother about keeping our physical body fit to look good and feel good but we don't bother to keep our mind fit and healthy.

Both physical and mental health is very crucial for us without which we cannot survive.

But if we are physically strong and mentally weak, it will be of no use because with a weak mind we can't achieve anything and be successful. A weak mind will attract more negativity and negative thoughts that will impact our growth, success and thus overall life.

If we are mentally strong and physically weak, it is also of no use as we need energy to do things.

When our body is physically healthy, it will absorb the positive energy available around us which is responsible for the proper functioning of our body.

So, a healthy body will create a healthy mind and a healthy mind will create a healthy body. Both are very important and should be taken care with equal importance.

A healthy mind will generate good thoughts and a healthy body will radiate positive energy.

Understanding these concepts of oneness of mind and oneness of universe and energy; applying it to our thoughts in managing our thoughts; implementing uniqueness in Thinking will help us become successful in life and will get us the results we want.

What we have seen in this book: Unique Thinking

Answers explained in detail for these questions.

❖ **What makes a Thought so powerful?**

- A Thought creates an identity to a person.
- A Thought is what we live in everyday.
- A Thought is what we execute everyday.
- A Thought is what makes us.
- A Thought is what makes our life.
- A Thought is a goal oriented flow of ideas resulting in reality oriented conclusion.
- A Thought is an idea or opinion produced by Thinking or sudden occurrence in the mind.

❖ **What is Thought Management?**

We all desire success in life and for this we need to manage our thoughts and adapt to organized and structured way of thinking so as to achieve the desired expected outcome.

This is what I Thought, to be called as Unique Thinking and Thought Management for attaining Uniqueness in thinking and establishing with our mind- the Unique Thought Process and Thought Lifecycle Management.

❖ What is a Dream?

A DREAM can be defined as the recollection of Thoughts that happened in the past or the vision of Thoughts that will happen in the Future.

A Thought put into action is what distinguishes a Dream from Reality.

❖ What is called Uniqueness?

Uniqueness is our very own nature and way of Thinking and acting upon anything or any given situation.

❖ Uniqueness Quotient

After all the unorganized and clumsy thinking, we get to the state where we start to feel that.

Yes! This is what I like or this is what I feel like doing or This is the Person I am or the Person I want to be. And that thought distinguishes us from others and that creates our **Uniqueness Quotient.**

❖ Uniqueness in Thinking UIT

The unique qualities hidden within us when we try to execute them in our life make us stand out unique and this process of realizing the potential hidden within us by way of thinking and perceiving about any given situation or surroundings is what is called Uniqueness in Thinking UIT.

❖ Unique Thought Process UTP

Distinguished Thinking and the Difference of Thinking from others; this way of execution of the Thought Process forms the Unique Thought Process. There are various phases defined for a Unique Thought Process.

❖ **How do we structure and organize our Thoughts so as to achieve the results or success we all dream about?**

To attain Organized or Structured Thinking, we need to initially attain a Positive Mindset.

Organized Thinking is the grouping of ideas in a structured hierarchy which when acted upon parallely or sequentially result in the expected outcome.

❖ **Did you ever realize that we can live the way we like because it is our life and it is none other than us who has designed the life the way it is and the way we are leading and living in it.**

I believe this is where the Leading and Managing of thoughts come into picture in organizing and synchronizing our desires and opinions with our thoughts and visions to make us live the life we like.

❖ **So what is making us think something and execute something and experience something else?**

We need to understand that only when we get the synchronicity between our thoughts and actions we will be able to achieve the desired outcome.

❖ **How do we develop our thinking in a way to get the results we want?**

To develop our thinking in a way for getting the results we want, firstly we need to have clarity of our thoughts; what we desire and what we don't desire in life.

Organized and Structured Thinking, Positive thought process, Meditation, self-awareness and self-realization help us in understanding this to a certain extent.

- **Did we ever realize that we consciously and unconsciously don't think in synchronization with our dreams?**

We must realize that DREAMS are our THOUGHTS unconsciously hidden in our mind. To get them to REALITY or ignore them is OUR CHOICE.

- **How do we achieve the state of Thoughtfulness?**

Thoughtfulness can be defined as being thoughtful rather than immersed in a large pool of thoughts.

Thoughtfulness state of mind is achieved when we are able to think productively that meets the needs of our problems and solutions to be achieved for those problems.

- **Have you ever realized how do you speak about a certain thing with somebody all of sudden?**

Our mind unconsciously reaches to the state of Mindfulness or Thoughtfulness where it generates or retrieves the thoughts or ideas relevant for the topic of discussion or situation.

- **Why do we need to just follow others and behave like how they want us to behave and live like how they want us to live?**

This happens when we don't have clarity of Thoughts as to what we want and what we want to become in life.

- **What is Thoughtlessness and how do we achieve the state of Thoughtlessness?**

Thoughtlessness is one of the highest levels of mind in which we reach to a state of calmness where there are no thoughts. This is next level higher to the level of Thoughtfulness.

❖ What causes these uniqueness of Thoughts and differences of interpretation of thoughts and thought process?

The levels of interpretation, analysis and inference differ based on our life experiences and dimensions of thought process.

Where do these thoughts come from?

Thoughts come from our past experiences and life and information stored in our mind and through external stimulation.

❖ How do we handle situations at personal level by ways of unique thinking?

Unique thinking is not a principle or a methodology but rather a practice that can be followed in every phase and every aspect of our life.

❖ How to improve our thinking capabilities?

We can improve our thinking capabilities through reading good books, informative articles and journals, meeting good people from our colleagues and friends and from our family.

Meditation practices also help in programming our mind and designing our thoughts. It provides the direction to our thoughts.

❖ How is it possible for the mind to retrieve the information from the universal mind?

We are already living in an abundant pool of knowledge. Our subconscious mind is our gateway for the universal intelligence. We need to have the capability to open the doors of our mind for accessing the data.

Brain is the visible organ of the human body while mind is the invisible organ existing within us. Each one of us is gifted with this miracle of mind.

Some of the methods and practices for achieving Unique thinking mindset

- Input of quality data into mind.
- Interacting with appropriate group of people.
- Improving the power of our mind through regular meditation practices.
- Listening to inspiring and motivational talks.
- Reading the biographies of successful people and learning from it.
- Allowing our mind to interact with the universal mind to achieve the capability of retrieving the abundantly available data around us.
- Understanding the concepts and relevance of the oneness of mind.
- Meeting spiritual and knowledgeable people and understanding things from their life and experiences.
- Adapting to a healthy lifestyle and healthy mindset through positive thinking practices.
- Realizing the importance of positivity and positive thinking in our life.
- Realizing and understanding the importance of designing and organizing our thoughts for executing them to get the required outcome.
- Memorizing the positive incidents we had come across in our life and remembering the positive minded people.

- Attaining the state of clarity of mind and calmness of mind through mind control and improvement techniques.

Stages of Thought Process

Thought Occurrence:

A Thought is an idea generated in the mind as a result of the stimulation from the surroundings or people surrounding us; or can be defined as a sudden recollection of our knowledge and experiences.

This Occurrence of Thought is the initial point of the Thought Process which stands as the starting point in the **Unique Thought Process.**

All of us get Thoughts every single second but they don't sustain in our minds or we don't remember what we think most of the times.

For these types of non-sustaining thoughts which don't have any impact on our Thought Process, Thought Occurrence and Thought Lapse stages occur consecutively one after the other.

Thought Sustenance:

Thought Sustenance forms the next stage of Thought Occurrence and only sustained thoughts enter this stage. We can consider it as the initiation of the Thought Process and Thought Management Life Cycle.

These sustained thoughts which we call it as **ideas** form the distinguishing **Factor of Change** in our life.

Thought Realization:

The sustained Thoughts move to the Thought Realization phase where we feel our ideas to be considered worthy and we feel like taking them forward and executing them. That feeling of importance we give to our ideas and thoughts is called Thought Realization.

Thought Organization and Design:

After we realize our thoughts, we tend to structure or organize our thoughts as per our requirements using some inferences of our surroundings, images, audio and video messages, our experiences and knowledge.

That means we are designing our Thoughts based on our needs and requirements.

Thought Execution:

After we structure our Thoughts in the required manner, we go with executing our Thought Design. This is when we take some action against our Thoughts to achieve the desired expected outcome.

Thought Outcome:

Thought Outcome is the result of the Thought Execution. So, Thought Design and Thought Execution form the key deciding factors for success or failure in life.

Thought Reoccurrence:

Thought Reoccurrence is the stage where we will be able to recollect all the previous thoughts clearly that have lead to the Thought Outcome which decides the result of any work or activity we do. So, Thought Execution forms the most important stage of the Thought Process.

Thought Continuity:

Thought Continuity is the phase wherein we get the flow of ideas or thoughts that help us achieve the expected outcome.

Thought Continuity can be a continuous process or it can start from Thought Occurrence for subsequent ideas and thoughts.

This phase continues until the expected outcome is achieved.

Thought Lapse:

Thought Lapse is the final stage of the Thought Process wherein we tend to forget our Thoughts and the Thought Process Cycle tends to fade away gradually with time and active engagement of our mind in other activities in life.

Unique Thinking Quotes

- A Thought creates an identity to a person.
- A Thought is what we live in everyday.
- A Thought is what we execute everyday.
- A Thought is what makes us.
- A Thought is what makes our life.
- A Thought is a goal oriented flow of ideas resulting in reality oriented conclusion.
- A Thought is an idea or opinion produced by Thinking or sudden occurrence in the mind.
- A Thought put into action is what distinguishes a Dream from Reality.
- Every individual's mind is engaged with Thoughts which take the form of actions that define our identity and recognition of a person.
- A Thought is a sudden occurrence in the mind based on our five sensory perceptions.

- Distinguished Thinking and the Difference of Thinking from others; Thought Process forms the Unique Thought Process UTP.
- Organized Thinking is all about how we can sequentially organize or prioritize or execute the elements of a Thought in a structure or hierarchy of Thought Process.
- This universe is made of energy and matter and Thought can be defined as the conversion of Energy into signals based on a particular frequency with which it vibrates at that level; which in turn creates the manifestation of images and vision upon thinking continuously will get materialized into Reality that we can see.
- Organized Thinking forms a significant phenomenon in the concept of Law of Thinking.
- Law of Thinking states that everything we see in Reality is the result of the materialization of the Manifested Visions and Thoughts.
- If the frequency of our Thoughts match with the frequency of Manifested Thoughts that were materialized in the past, we will be able to recollect those incidents or Thoughts which we call as Memories.
- If the frequency of our thoughts match with the frequency of incidents that are going to take place in Future, we get the vision of those incidents.
- Belief can be defined as the Thought of our Mind that emerges from our experiences as a result of our actions in our past or events in our future.
- First we need to state our mind what we want and then ask it how to achieve it and then program it

with the required information and knowledge and then allow it to work for us.

- We develop efficiency and capabilities within us based on our thoughts and experiences in life.
- Dreams are nothing but the visions and thoughts of your inner desires to be materialized and manifested into Reality.
- All that we need to do is think in synchronicity with our dreams.
- We must realize that DREAMS are our THOUGHTS unconsciously hidden in our mind. To get them to REALITY or ignore them is OUR CHOICE.
- Reprogram your mind with a Unique belief system. Believe that anything is possible.
- We live by our Thoughts and we lead our lives by our Thoughts which implies we are made by our Thoughts.
- Thoughts define us and our lives and mastering the art of Thought Management and adapting to Uniqueness of Thoughts will help us master ourselves and our lives.
- What matters is how we apply this thought management and concepts of Uniqueness of thoughts in thinking different from others.
- We are what we Think.

Some Facts about the brain

1) An adult brain weighs about 3 pounds.

2) About 75 percent of the brain is made up of water. This means that dehydration, even in small amounts, can have a negative effect on the brain functions.

3) The largest brain of any animal is that of the sperm whale. It weighs about 20 pounds.

4) Signs of successful brain surgeries go as far back as the Stone Age.

5) The human brain will grow three times its size in the first year of life. It continues to grow until you're about 18 years old.

6) Headaches are caused by a chemical reaction in your brain combined with the muscles and nerves of your neck and head.

7) The brain of a human contains approximately one hundred billion neurons

9) Cholesterol is useful for learning and memory. However, high cholesterol has different effects depending on your age and other factors.

10) Information runs between neurons in your brain for everything we see, think, or do. These neurons move information at different speeds. The fastest speed for information to pass between neurons is about 250 mph.

11) Dreams are believed to be a combination of imagination, psychological factors, and eurological factors. They prove that your brain is working even when you are sleeping.

12) Phantom limb pain syndrome is when the central nervous system, which includes your brain, continues to feel the pain of a limb that has been amputated.

13) The brain can't feel pain. It interprets pain signals sent to it, but it does not feel pain.

14) A brain freeze is really a sphenopalatine ganglioneuralgia. It happens when something you eat or drink something that's cold. It chills the blood vessels and arteries in the very back of the throat, including the ones that take blood to your brain. These constrict when they're cold and open back up with they're warm again, causing the pain in your forehead.

15) The human brain begins to lose some memory abilities as well as some cognitive skills by your late 20s.

16) The human brain gets smaller as we get older. This usually happens sometime after middle age.

17) During the mummification process, Egyptians would usually remove the brains through the nose.

18) Alcohol effects your brain in ways that include blurred vision, slurred speaking, an unsteady walk, and more. These usually disappear once you become sober again. However, if you drink often for long periods of time, there is evidence that alcohol can affect your brain permanently and not reverse once you become sober again. Long term effects include memory issues and some reduced cognitive function.

19) Eyewitness accounts of criminal suspects is usually only about 50 percent accurate because it is difficult for your brain to remember the details of

someone you're not familiar with. Traumatic events can also affect the brains ability to remember details.

20) Computer or video games may help improve cognitive abilities. However, more studies must be conducted to learn how much they help or what types of games help.

21) Your brain uses 20 percent of the oxygen and blood in your body.

Brain Matter

Brain is made up of billions of neurons (or nerve cells) that communicate in trillions of connections called synapses, your brain is one of the most complex and fascinating organs in your body. Keeping your brain healthy and active is vital. Discover just how powerful it is with these interesting facts.

1. Sixty percent of the human brain is made of fat. Not only does that make it the fattiest organ in the human body, but these fatty acids are crucial for your brain's performance. Make sure you're fueling it appropriately with healthy, brain-boosting nutrients.

2. Your brain isn't fully formed until age 25. Brain development begins from the back of the brain and works its way to the front. Therefore, your frontal lobes, which control planning and reasoning, are the last to strengthen and structure connections.

3. Your brain's storage capacity is considered virtually unlimited. Research suggests the human brain consists of about 86 billion neurons. Each neuron forms connections to other neurons, which could add up to 1 quadrillion (1,000 trillion) connections. Over time, these neurons can combine, increasing

storage capacity. However, in Alzheimer's disease, for example, many neurons can become damaged and stop working, particularly affecting memory.

4. Brain information travels up to an impressive 268 miles per hour. When a neuron is stimulated, it generates an electrical impulse that travels from cell to cell. A disruption in this regular processing can cause an epileptic seizure.

5. On average, your spinal cord stops growing at 4 years old. Your spinal cord, which consists of a bundle of nervous tissue and support cells, is responsible for sending messages from your brain throughout your body.

6. The spinal cord is the main source of communication between the body and the brain. ALS, or amyotrophic lateral sclerosis, causes the neurons in the brain and spinal cord to die, impacting controlled muscle movement. Another disease that affects both the brain and the spinal cord is multiple sclerosis (MS). In MS, the immune system attacks the protective layer that covers nerve fibers, causing communication problems between the brain and the body.

7. Neurologists confirm that your brain is always active even while sleeping.

8. The human brain can generate about 23 watts of power (enough to power a lightbulb). All that power calls for some much-needed rest. Adequate sleep helps maintain the pathways in your brain. Additionally, sleep deprivation can increase the build-up of a protein in your brain that is linked to Alzheimer's disease.

Your brain has a big job. Be sure to take care of it.

Our brains allow us to process the world, understand everything around us, learn new things, and paradoxically, we're still very unaware of how much of our own brains function. However, modern neuroscience and cognitive sciences have made great strides in understanding the effect our brains have on our everyday functions.

With that, comes a wealth of knowledge and a variety of facts that you probably don't know about the brain.

Interesting stories about the human brain

1. Nearly all colors have a physical wavelength associated with it, but the color Magenta doesn't. Rather, your brain is simply processing the color as "not green."

2. When you find yourself sleeping in a new environment for the first time, the brain processes danger and remains half-awake in order to be more aware.

3. A man by the name of Bruce Bridgeman spent nearly his entire life, 67 years, without the ability of depth perception, called stereoblindness. However, after being forced to purchase 3D glasses to watch the movie Hugo in theaters, his brain clicked and he was able to experience 3D vision.

4. A man in the UK had chronic hiccups for 2.5 years of his life and was told that it was likely caused by heartburn. After a Japanese TV show picked up the strange phenomena and paid for medical testing, a brain tumor was discovered. Once the man had the tumor removed, his chronic hiccups went away for good.

5. Blacking out from drinking is actually caused by the effect of alcohol on the hippocampus, the part

of your brain responsible for memory. You're not physically forgetting anything, rather your brain becomes incapable of storing and recording new memories.

6. We cry when we are very happy because our hypothalamus in our brain can't distinguish the difference between strong happiness and strong sadness.

7. We get chills when we listen to music as a result of our brain releasing dopamine. When a song "moves" you, the anticipation from a peak moment in the song triggers this release.

8. Solitary confinement can actually cause extreme neurological damage to human brains. So much so that it can be seen on EEG scans and the brains of solitary prisoners have the same indicators as people who have had traumatic injuries.

9. While we sleep, our spinal fluid flows through the brain on the outside of the brain's blood vessels. This removes brain cell waste, specific buildups of amyloid-beta protein. This only occurs during sleep and a buildup of the proteins that get cleaned has been linked to greater risks of Alzheimer's.

10. A scientist by the name of Theodor Erismann created goggles that completely flip his vision. At first, he struggled with the flipped perception, but within just 5 days, his brain adapted to the change and he saw everything as normal. This type of adaptation is also well demonstrated by YouTuber "Smarter Every Day" who forgot how to ride a bike and relearned flipped his bike steering around, causing him to forget how to ride a bike and relearn in a reverse manner.

11. Alzheimer's disease is caused by a resistance to insulin in the brain, causing many to refer to it as type 3 diabetes.

12. The world's fastest supercomputer requires 24 million Watts of power to operate, but our brains only require 20 Watts and operate about 100,000 times faster.

13. Exercise slows our brains' cognitive decline and increased physical activity over the norm can slow our brain's aging by 10 years.

14. Human brains receive 20% of the total oxygen from our bodies even though they only represent 2% of our bodies' weight.

15. Certain languages do not have terms for Left, Right, Front, Back, and rather use the terms North, South, East, West. People raised in these languages have been found to always know what direction they are oriented, resulting in a type of compass brain.

16. 73% of your brain is just water, which means that if you get dehydrated by more than 2%, you can suffer from a loss in attention, cognitive skills, and memory.

17. Babies' brains grow rapidly. A 2-year-old baby will have an 80% fully grown brain. This rapid development is why paying close attention to your child's development in the early years is so impactful to their ability as an adult.

18. Information transfer in our brain occurs at a rate equivalent to 260 miles per hour.

19. Yawning is actually a reaction that sends more oxygen to your brain. Reptiles, birds, and mammals all yawn and it's controlled by neurotransmitters in the brain.

20. The cerebellum is the part of the brain responsible for posture, walking, and movement coordination. It is located in the back of the brain and weighs 150 grams.

21. The human brain is split into two sides, with each interacting with the opposite side of the body. While this interaction is known, the reason for it is still not understood.

22. Within your brain, there are 150,000 miles of blood vessels that carry blood and oxygen to various parts of the organ.

23. You can actually improve your memory if you choose to eat seafood regularly. The fatty acids in these foods improve the memory storing parts of your brain.

24. The human brain continues to develop until your late 40s. It is the only organ in the body that develops for this long of a time – and it sees more changes than any other organ as well.

25. Every second, there are 100,000 chemical reactions happening in the human brain.

26. Babies lose about half of their neurons before they are born. Referred to as pruning, this eliminates any brain neurons that don't receive sufficient input from other areas of the brain.

27. Studies have found that when mothers speak to their babies, the children learned, on average, 300 more words by the age of 2.

28. EEGs or electroencephalograms is a non-invasive imaging technique that is used to record small changes of electrical activity in the brain. Utilizing surface electrodes on the scalp, scientists can study many aspects of the brain utilizing this technique. Tiny fluctuations in the EEG signals indicate whether a person is asleep, aroused, or somewhere in-between.

29. Researchers from Baylor University have discovered that children who are deprived of touch, play, and interaction with others have 20-30% smaller brains than what is normal for their age. Child abuse can thus inhibit brain development in a child and negatively affect their lifetime brain development.

30. The brain cannot experience pain. This allows neurosurgeons to probe areas within the brain while patients are awake. They can then get real-time feedback from each patient, allowing them to pinpoint particular regions, like for speech or movement.

31. The reaction of our pupils constricting when they are exposed to bright light is called the pupillary light reflex. This reflex is used by doctors to determine whether the reflex pathway to the brain has been disrupted. If one or both of your eyes fail to produce this reflex, then doctors can work to pinpoint the exact location of the disconnect.

32. 5% of the population of the world has epilepsy. However, it's estimated that 1 in 10 people will have a seizure within their lifetime.

33. Every time that you remember something, you, in turn, strengthen that memory in your brain. Whenever the neural pathways of a memory are

exercised, your brain makes new connections. The older and more times a memory has been remembered, the stronger that memory is.

34. During sleep, your body produces a hormone that prevents you from getting up and acting out your dreams. Five minutes after a dream, your body has already forgotten half of it and ten minutes later it is 90% gone from your memory.

35. Our brains can compute 10 to the 13th and 10 to the 16th operations per second. That is equivalent to 1 million times the people on earth. In theory, brains are capable of solving problems faster than any computer in the world, perhaps better than any computer that will ever exist.

36. Good nutrition is incredibly important to brain health. Dieting can force the brain to start eating itself and malnourished fetuses or infants can suffer from cognitive and behavioral deficits. Babies need proper nourishment because their brains use up to 50% of their total glucose supply, another reason why they may need so much sleep.

37. Humans experience 70,000 thoughts each day.

38. Our sense of smell is the only sense that is directly linked to our limbic system. This part of the brain specializes in physical, emotional, and psychological responses. This all means that good smells can change our moods drastically in a snap.

39. A group of researchers studied London Taxi drivers and found that they had a larger hippocampus, the part of the brain responsible for memory. This suggests that the more you are forced to memorize, the larger this part of your brain grows.

40. Making music may actually have a quantifiable effect on our brain. When you hook up guitar players to electrodes, researchers discovered that brainwaves of musicians synchronize when they play duets.

41. The average weight of brains for men is 2.9 pounds and for women 2.6 pounds. However, that doesn't correlate to higher intelligence. For example, Einstein's brain weighed 2.7 pounds.

42. The brain is the only object in the world that can contemplate itself.

43. Chronic exposer to stress actually overloads your brain with hormones that are only intended for short-term emergency functions. In turn, that means that long-term exposure can kill brain cells.

44. Of people ages 1 to 44, traumatic brain injury is the leading cause of disability and death. Most commonly involved are falls, motor vehicle crashes, and assaults.

45. The average size of the human brain has decreased by 9 cubic inches over a period of the last 5000 years. Scientists aren't exactly sure why.

46. Déjà vu(the feeling that a new event has already been experienced or that the same scene has been witnessed before) hasn't been fully explained. Scientists think that it's actually a neurological glitch caused by something being registered in memory before conscious thought.

47. What seems like random light when you hit your head, is actually just jolts to brain cells responsible for vision. These visual "hallucinations" are just simple responses.

Interesting things about the brain, psychology & the mind

1. Brain can store an estimated 2,500,000 gigabytes

According to Paul Reber, Professor of Psychology at Northwestern University, the human brain can store an estimated 2,500,000 gigabytes. That's equivalent to 300 years worth of TV shows.

2. The human attention span is shorter than a goldfish

Research shows that the average attention span has decreased by an average 12 minutes over the last 10 years. Today, the human attention span is shorter than a goldfish. Studies have even shown some links between device multi-tasking — for example, if you're scrolling through social media while watching TV — and declining attention spans.

3. The average weight of the adult human brain is three pounds

On average, the adult brain weighs three pounds. For reference, this is comparable to how much a cantaloupe weighs.

4. Memories are stored for both short-term and long-term use at the same time

Neuroscientists have known for a long time that the hippocampus stores short-term memories. However, a recent study revealed that while short-term memories are formed in the hippocampus, they are simultaneously stored in another part of the brain for long-term memories.

5. Vitamin B1 can help improve short- and long-term memory

Vitamin B1 is essential to producing the brain chemical acetylcholine, which is needed for concentrating and storing memories. An Australian study revealed that those who consumed B1 supplements and folic acid for two years improved long and short-term memory.

6. Easy access to information can make it harder to remember

Being able to quickly access information–i.e. via our borderline invincible Internet—actually makes it harder to remember. The harder we work to access data, the more likely we are to remember.

7. Memories start forming in the womb

Memories start forming in the womb, as this is a critical time for brain development. Memory recall can occur as early as four months into pregnancy.

8. Brain uses 20% of the body's total oxygen and energy

The brain uses 20 percent of the body's total oxygen and energy, which travels to the brain through blood vessels. Nerve cells in the brain need a lot of energy; without adequate oxygen and energy to the central nervous system tissue, one can suffer impaired brain functions and neurological disorders.

9. Brain is composed of 73% water

The brain is 73 percent water. It only takes 2 percent dehydration to affect your attention and memory.

10. Sweating can temporarily shrink the brain

An hour and a half of sweating can temporarily shrink brain size as much as one year of aging does.

11. Five minutes without oxygen can cause brain damage

Five minutes without oxygen can lead to brain cells dying, which causes brain damage.

12. It generates 12-15 watts of electricity

The brain generates between 12 and 25 watts of electricity—that's enough to power a low wattage light bulb!

13. Neurons travel 150 mph in the brain

Neurons travel 150 mph in the brain. Different types of neurons move at different speeds - for example, pain signals move much slower than other ones.

14. Those who take a quiz twice are 65% more likely to remember the facts

Those who take a quiz after its revision are 65 percent more likely to remember the facts.

15. Learning new things increases gray matter in the brain

When we learn something new, our brain forms new connections between neurons; this then increases visible gray matter in the brain.

16. Memory is prioritized by emotion

Memory is prioritized by emotion. But this also means that a lot of our "memories" are unintended flawed fiction.

17. Emotions can alter our brain chemistry

Similarly to the above fact, emotions drastically alter our brains. The chemical reactions stirred by feelings can be physically seen in brain scans and studies of gray matter.

18. It has an average of 50,000-70,000 thoughts a day

The average brain has between 50,000 and 70,000 thoughts a day. Upsettingly, the majority (an estimated 60-70 percent) of the thoughts are negative.

19. More than 100,000 chemical reactions take place in the brain every second

With roughly 100 billion brain cells, more than 100,000 chemical reactions take place in the brain every second.

20. When intoxicated, it can't form memories

When intoxicated, the brain is incapable of forming memories. So no, you didn't "forget" what happened last night. The memory simply was never formed.

21. Practicing recollection can help PTSD

Practicing recollection can help aid PTSD. There are a variety of psychological treatment methods that mental health care providers use to help those suffering from PTSD safely confront and cope with traumatic experiences.

22. Brain texture and consistency is comparable to tofu. This isn't too surprising, given that it's made up primarily of gray and white matter, as well as water.

23. It starts slowing at around 24 years old

Research shows that the cognitive speed of your brain starts slowing down when you're around 24 years old.

24. 95% of all decisions are subconscious

95 percent of all decisions take place in the subconscious mind. This means that the vast majority of our actions and behaviors occur due to brain activity that lies beyond our conscious awareness.

25. The brain itself cannot feel pain

Although pain is processed in the brain, the organ itself cannot feel pain. This is why brain surgeries can occur while a patient is awake, without discomfort.

The list goes on and on. As more research is conducted, and we learn more about the human brain's capabilities, we also learn how to keep our minds sharp. Find out how we recall memories and how the brain changes when you learn.

As good as the brain is at turning short-term memories into long-term ones, it's still important to keep those memories preserved for future generations. That's why Legacybox helps you to digitize your memories - whether you have tapes, film, photos, or audio recordings, we're here to help.

Psychology Facts About Love and Relationships

1. When lovers look into each others' eyes, their heartbeats synchronize.
2. If you want someone to like you, ask for their help. The Ben Franklin Effect shows that by asking someone for help, you're instilling confidence in them and initiating trust, which makes them try harder to like you.
3. People who are similarly rated in attractiveness often end up together.
4. It takes only four minutes to decide if you like someone or not.
5. Some animals do, in fact, mate for life. Those include: Gibbons, swans, beavers and otters
6. Cuddling can be used as a painkiller.

7. Similarly, looking at a loved one can also be used to dull pain.

8. Broken Heart Syndrome is a real phenomenon experienced when you're so emotionally distraught that you have chest pain.

9. Being in love lowers your stress by upping your serotonin levels.

10. Allowing yourself to experience the negative emotions of an event in your life might actually help you move past it faster

Psychology Facts About Learning, Thinking and Studying

11. Writing notes longhand, instead of typing them, helps you learn what you're notating because writing engages a different part of the brain than typing.

12. You might learn more by listening to music when you study. Listening to music helps you engage the parts of your brain that help you focus.

13. Higher expectations leads to better performance, The Pygmalion Effect and Rosenthal Effects explain it best, but the idea is that teachers pay more attention to students they know are more likely to succeed.

14. There are four major reasons you're forgetful – failure to retrieve, interference, failure to store and intentional deletion.

15. Thinking through decisions in a foreign language helps take the emotion out of your thoughts and helps you focus on making a more rational decision.

16. Need to improve your memory? You need to strengthen you synapses. The best ways to do that are: avoid stress, drugs and alcohol and get plenty of sleep and exercise.

17. Reading notes aloud (and talking to yourself about the material) helps you learn more.

18. Playing Chess makes you smarter – it slows you down and forces you to concentrate. Chess also relies on players to think through things from various angles – they must use both deductive and inductive thinking.
19. Playing with blocks helps younger children with learning because it teaches spatial concepts, as well as physics.

Random Psychology Facts

19. The color blue is an appetite suppressant

20. A study actually found that playing video games can have some good side effects on kids, too. Video games gives kids a chance to unleash their negative emotions and also to face and defeat scary things.

21. No one born blind has ever developed schizophrenia.

22. You might think it's the opposite, but announcing your goals to others actually demotivates you and makes you less likely to meet your goal.

23. Think your personality changes over time? You're partially right. It's been proven that your core personality traits don't change as you age. However, over time your anxiety levels, friendliness and bravery for trying new things can flux multiple times depending on experiences and trauma related to those experiences.

24. Spending money on others makes you happier than spending money on yourself.
25. Ever get frustrated during a Facebook argument when someone only links to sources supporting their claim, even if those sources are sketchy AF? Called "Confirmation bias," the idea is that people will always be drawn to and more readily stand by "facts" that confirm what they already believe to be true.
26. Humans tend to care more about one person than about massive tragedies.
27. During a crying sesh, if the first teardrop comes from the right eye, that person is crying tears of joy. If from the left, the person is crying tears of pain.
28. Having a plan B means plan A is less likely to work.
29. The beginning and end of a story are easier to remember than the middle.
30. It takes up to five positive things to outweigh one single negative thing.
31. We care about ourselves more than others, which is why the reward part of the brain lights up when we're talking about ourselves.
32. Babies start processing language like adults do as soon as they're two days old.
33. Moving their mouths helps babies listen.
34. Babies consolidate memories and new learned skills while they sleep, which is why napping is so important especially in the first year of their life.

Gifted thoughts:

Management and Leadership Quotes

1. Management is the opportunity to help people become better. Practiced that way, it's a magnificent profession.

   - Clayton M. Christensen

2. Management's job is to convey leadership's message in a compelling and inspiring way. Not just in meetings, but also by example

   - Jeffrey Gitomer

3. Good management consists in showing average people how to do the work of superior people

   - John D. Rockefeller

4. Management is about arranging and telling. Leadership is about nurturing and enhancing.

   - Tom Peters

5. Growth makes so many dimensions of management easier. It's when growth stops that things get tough.

6. Management is, above all, a practice where art, science, and craft meet."

   - Henry Mintzberg

7. "If you are the master be sometimes blind, if you are the servant be sometimes deaf."

   - R Buckminster Fuller

8. "The conventional definition of management is getting work done through people, but real management is developing people through work."

- Agha Hasan Abedi

9. “Keep on going, and the chances are that you will stumble on something, perhaps when you are least expecting it. I never heard of anyone ever stumbling on something sitting down.”

- Charles F. Kettering

10. “Don’t be intimidated by what you don’t know. That can be your greatest strength and ensure that you do things differently from everyone else.”

- Sara Blakely

11. A leader is best when people barely know he exists, when his work is done, his aim fulfilled, they will say: we did it ourselves.”

- Lao Tzu

12. “One’s philosophy is not best expressed in words; it is expressed in the choices one makes—and the choices we make are ultimately our responsibility.”

- Eleanor Roosevelt

13. “The ultimate measure of a man is not where he stands in the moments of comfort, but where he stands at times of challenge and controversy.”

- Martin Luther King, Jr.

14. “Behind every great man is a woman rolling her eyes.”

- Jim Carrey

15. “Leaders aren’t born, they are made. And they are made just like anything else, through hard work. And that’s the price we’ll have to pay to achieve that goal, or any goal.”

- Vince Lombardi

16. “My philosophy has always been, if you can put staff first, your customer second and shareholders third, effectively, in the end, the shareholders do well, the customers do better, and you’re happy.”

- Richard Branson

17. “It’s better to hang out with people better than you. Pick out associates whose behavior is better than yours and you’ll drift in that direction.”

- Warren Buffett

18. “The two most powerful warriors are patience and time...so remember: great achievements take time, there is no overnight success.”

- Leo Tolstoy

19. “You’ve got enemies? Good, that means you stood up for something in your life.”

- Eminem

20. There is a very clear distinction between Leadership and Management

    With Management you tell people what to do, Leaders inspire them to do it

    Inspiration is the key here

    There are 3 components to true inspiration

    Clarity of vision

    Courage of your convictions

Ability to effectively communicate

You have to believe in what you are doing with truly every fiber of your being.

You must have the clarity of your vision and the courage of your conviction to be able to evangelize in a way that people can easily understand what it is that you are trying to accomplish and can act upon it

- Jeff Weiner , LinkedIn

21. "If your actions create a legacy that inspire others to dream more, learn more, do more and become more, then, you are an excellent leader."

- Dolly Parton

22. "Delegating work works, provided the one delegating works, too."

- Robert Half

23. Followers think and talk about their problems.... Leaders think and talk about the solutions."

- Brian Tracy

24. Those who let things happen usually lose to those who make things happen.

- Dave Weinbaum

25. A man who wants to lead the orchestra must turn his back on the crowd.

- Max Lucado

26. A teacher affects eternity; he can never tell where his influence stops.

- Henry Adams

27. People buy into the leader before they buy into the vision.

- John C. Maxwell

28. A company is stronger if it is bound by love rather than by fear.

- Herb Kelleher

29. The key to successful leadership today is influence, not authority.

- Kenneth Blanchard

30. To lead people, walk behind them.

- Lao Tzu

31. As we look ahead into the next century, leaders will be those who empower others.

- Bill Gates

32. He who has great power should use it lightly.

- Seneca

33. Leadership cannot just go along to get along. Leadership must meet the moral challenge of the day.

- Jesse Jackson

34. The art of leadership is saying no, not yes. It is very easy to say yes.

- Tony Blair

35. Don't follow the crowd, let the crowd follow you.

- Margaret Thatcher

36. Leadership and learning are indispensable to each other.

- John F. Kennedy

37. Leadership is the art of giving people a platform for spreading ideas that work.

- Seth Godin

38. Innovation distinguishes between a leader and a follower.

- Steve Jobs

39. Leadership is unlocking people's potential to become better

- Bill Bradley

40. A cowardly leader is the most dangerous of men.

- Stephen King

41. No man is good enough to govern another man without that other's consent."

- Abraham Lincoln

42. There are three essentials to leadership: humility, clarity and courage."

- Fuchan Yuan

43. Not the cry, but the flight of a wild duck, leads the flock to fly and follow."

- Chinese Proverb

44. To add value to others, one must first value others."

- John C. Maxwell

45. If one is lucky, a solitary fantasy can totally transform one million realities."

- Maya Angelou

46. Leadership does not always wear the harness of compromise."

- Woodrow Wilson

47. The greatest leaders mobilize others by coalescing people around a shared vision."

- Ken Blanchard

48. "To do great things is difficult; but to command great things is more difficult."

- Friedrich Nietzsche

49. The first key to leadership is self-control.

- Jack Weatherford

50. Earn your leadership every day.

- Michael Jordan

51. The growth and development of people is the highest calling of leadership.

- Harvey Firestone

52. A leader takes people where they would never go on their own.

- Hans Finzel

53. The supreme quality of leadership is integrity.

- Dwight D. Eisenhower

54. I suppose leadership at one time meant muscles; but today it means getting along with people.

- Mahatma Gandhi

55. Leadership is about taking responsibility, not making excuses.

- Mitt Romney

56. The quality of a leader is reflected in the standards they set for themselves.

- Ray Kroc

57. A good plan violently executed now is better than a perfect plan executed next week.

- George Patton

58. The speed of the leader is the speed of the group.

- Mary Kay Ash

59. Great companies in the way they work, start with great leaders.

- Steve Ballmer

60. Great leaders are willing to sacrifice the numbers to save the people.

- Simon Sinek

61. Anyone can hold the helm when the sea is calm.

- Publilius Syrus

62. A great person attracts great people and knows how to hold them together.

- Johann Wolfgang Von Goethe

63. I am reminded how hollow the label of leadership sometimes is and how heroic followership can be.

- Warren Bennis

64. Become the kind of leader that people would follow voluntarily; even if you had no title or position.

- Brian Tracy

65. When eagles are silent, parrots begin to chatter.

- Winston Churchill

66. Don't necessarily avoid sharp edges. Occasionally they are necessary to leadership.

- Donald Rumsfeld

67. Real leaders are ordinary people with extraordinary determinations.

- John Seaman Garns

68. If you really want the key to success, start by doing the opposite of what everyone else is doing.

- Brad Szollose

69. You get the best efforts from others not by lighting a fire beneath them, but by building a fire within.

- Bob Nelson

70. A leader's job is to look into the future and see the organization, not as it is, but as it should be.

- Jack Welch

71. You get in life what you have the courage to ask for.

- Nancy D. Solomon

72. A leader is someone who creates infectious enthusiasm.

- Ted Turner

73. Leadership is the capacity to translate vision into reality.

- Warren Bennis

74. You do not lead by hitting people over the head - that's assault, not leadership.

- Dwight D. Eisenhower

75. I cannot trust a man to control others who cannot control himself.

- Robert E. Lee

76. Great leaders state out loud what they intend to do and in doing so, they get things done.

77. Great leaders inspire people to have confidence in themselves.

- Eleanor Roosevelt

78. Business leaders cannot be bystanders.

- Howard Schultz

79. Leadership is not about titles, positions, or flowcharts. It is about one life influencing another.

- John C. Maxwell

80. If you spend your life trying to be good at everything, you will never be great at anything.

- Tom Rath

81. What you do has far greater impact than what you say.

- Stephen Covey

82. The most common way people give up their power is by thinking they don't have any.

- Alice Walker

83. If you want to lift yourself up, lift up someone else.

- Booker T. Washington

84. To command is to serve, nothing more and nothing less.

- Andre Malraux

85. Leadership is intentional influence.

- Michael McKinney

86. A great leader's courage to fulfill his vision comes from passion, not position.

- John C. Maxwell

87. Trust is the essence of Leadership.

- Colin Powell

88. A real leader faces the music even when he doesn't like the tune.

- Arnold H. Glasgow

89. When people are placed in positions slightly above what they expect, they are apt to excel.

- Richard Branson

90. The real leader has no need to lead — he is content to point the way.

- Henry Miller

91. A leader is a dealer in hope.

- Napoleon Bonaparte

92. The task of the leader is to get his people from where they are to where they have not been.

- Henry Kissinger

93. Leadership is the art of accomplishing more than what the science of management says is possible.

- Colin Powell

94. Education is the mother of leadership

- Wendell Willkie

95. Leadership is the key to 99 percent of all successful efforts.

- Erskine Bowles

96. Ninety percent of leadership is the ability to communicate something people want.

- Dianne Feinstein

97. A good leader can't get too far ahead of his followers.

- Franklin D. Roosevelt

98. You take people as far as they will go, not as far as you would like them to go.

- Jeanette Rankin

99. Leadership has a harder job to do than just choose sides. It must bring sides together

- Jesse Jackson

100. The first responsibility of a leader is to define reality

- Max De Pree

101. Leaders don't force people to follow—they invite them on a journey.

- Charles S. Lauer

102. Leadership is getting someone to do what they don't want to do, to achieve what they want to achieve.

- Tom Landry

103. A good leader leads the people from above them. A great leader leads the people from within them.

- M.D. Arnold

104. Whenever you see a successful business, someone once made a courageous decision.

- Peter F. Drucker

105. Management works in the system; leadership works on the system.

- Stephen Covey

106. Example is not the main thing in influencing others. It is the only thing.

- Albert Schweitzer

107. Keep your fears to yourself, but share your courage with others.

- Robert L. Stevenson

108. Our chief want is someone who will inspire us to be what we know we could be.

- Ralph Waldo Emerson

109. To handle yourself, use your head; to handle others, use your heart.

- Eleanor Roosevelt

110. A leader is one who knows the way, goes the way and shows the way.

- John C. Maxwell

111. Leadership is an action, not a position.

- Donald McGannon

112. Surround yourself with great people; delegate authority; get out of the way.

- Ronald Reagan

113. Do not follow where the path may lead. Go instead where there is no path and leave a trail

- Ralph Waldo Emerson

114. The true mark of a leader is the willingness to stick with a bold course of action — an unconventional business strategy, a unique product-development roadmap, a controversial marketing campaign — even as the rest of the world wonders why you're not marching in step with the status quo. In other

words, real leaders are happy to zig while others zag. They understand that in an era of hyper-competition and non-stop disruption, the only way to stand out from the crowd is to stand for something special.

- Bill Taylor

115. Leaders instill in their people a hope for success and a belief in themselves. Positive leaders empower people to accomplish their goals.

- Unknown

116. The very essence of leadership is that you have to have vision. You can't blow an uncertain trumpet.

- Theodore M. Hesburgh

117. A good objective of leadership is to help those who are doing poorly to do well and to help those who are doing well to do even better.

- Jim Rohn

118. The single biggest way to impact an organization is to focus on leadership development. There is almost no limit to the potential of an organization that recruits good people, raises them up as leaders and continually develops them.

- John Maxwell

119. The pessimist complains about the wind. The optimist expects it to change. The leader adjusts the sails.

- John Maxwell

120. A leader is best when people barely know he exists, when his work is done, his aim fulfilled, they will say: we did it ourselves.

- Lao Tzu

121. The first responsibility of a leader is to define reality. The last is to say thank you. In between, the leader is a servant.

- Max DePree

122. Leadership is the capacity to translate vision into reality.

- Warren Bennis

123. Lead me, follow me, or get out of my way.

- General George Patton

124. Before you are a leader, success is all about growing yourself. When you become a leader, success is all about growing others.

- Jack Welch

125. You don't need a title to be a leader.

- Multiple Attributions

126. A leader is one who knows the way, goes the way, and shows the way.

- John Maxwell

127. My own definition of leadership is this: The capacity and the will to rally men and women to a common purpose and the character which inspires confidence.

- General Montgomery

128. Leadership is lifting a person's vision to high sights, the raising of a person's performance to a higher standard, the building of a personality beyond its normal limitations.

- Peter Drucker

129. Never doubt that a small group of thoughtful, concerned citizens can change the world. Indeed it is the only thing that ever has.

- Margaret Mead

130. The nation will find it very hard to look up to the leaders who are keeping their ears to the ground.

- Sir Winston Churchill

131. The most dangerous leadership myth is that leaders are born-that there is a genetic factor to leadership. That's nonsense; in fact, the opposite is true. Leaders are made rather than born.

- Warren Bennis

132. He who has never learned to obey cannot be a good commander.

- Aristotle

133. I start with the premise that the function of leadership is to produce more leaders, not more followers.

- Ralph Nader

134. Effective leadership is not about making speeches or being liked; leadership is defined by results not attributes.

- Peter Drucker

135. A great person attracts great people and knows how to hold them together.

- Johann Wolfgang Von Goethe

136. The best executive is the one who has sense enough to pick good men to do what he wants done, and self-restraint enough to keep from meddling with them while they do it.

- Theodore Roosevelt

137. Leadership is influence.

- John C. Maxwell

138. You don't lead by pointing and telling people some place to go. You lead by going to that place and making a case.

- Ken Kesey

139. When I give a minister an order, I leave it to him to find the means to carry it out.

- Napoleon Bonaparte

140. Men make history and not the other way around. In periods where there is no leadership, society stands still. Progress occurs when courageous, skillful leaders seize the opportunity to change things for the better.

- Harry S. Truman

141. People buy into the leader before they buy into the vision.

- John Maxwell

142. So much of what we call management consists in making it difficult for people to work.

- Peter Drucker

143. The key to successful leadership today is influence, not authority.

- Kenneth Blanchard

144. A good general not only sees the way to victory; he also knows when victory is impossible.

- Polybius

145. The challenge of leadership is to be strong, but not rude; be kind, but not weak; be bold, but not bully; be thoughtful, but not lazy; be humble, but not timid; be proud, but not arrogant; have humor, but without folly.

- Jim Rohn

146. Outstanding leaders go out of their way to boost the self-esteem of their personnel. If people believe in themselves, it's amazing what they can accomplish.

- Sam Walton

147. A true leader has the confidence to stand alone, the courage to make tough decisions, and the compassion to listen to the needs of others. He does not set out to be a leader, but becomes one by the equality of his actions and the integrity of his intent.

- Douglas MacArthur

148. A ruler should be slow to punish and swift to reward.

- Ovid

149. No man will make a great leader who wants to do it all by himself, or to get all the credit for doing it.

- Andrew Carnegie

150. Leadership is the art of getting someone else to do something you want done because he wants to do it.

- General Dwight Eisenhower

151. The leader has to be practical and a realist yet must talk the language of the visionary and the idealist.

- Eric Hoffer

152. Leaders think and talk about the solutions. Followers think and talk about the problems.

- Brian Tracy

153. A man who wants to lead the orchestra must turn his back on the crowd.

- Max Lucado

154. Never tell people how to do things. Tell them what to do and they will surprise you with their ingenuity.

- General George Patton

155. As we look ahead into the next century, leaders will be those who empower others.

- Bill Gates

156. All of the great leaders have had one characteristic in common: it was the willingness to confront unequivocally the major anxiety of their people in their time. This, and not much else, is the essence of leadership.

- John Kenneth Galbraith

157. Do what you feel in your heart to be right–for you'll be criticized anyway.

- Eleanor Roosevelt

158. Effective leadership is putting first things first. Effective management is discipline, carrying it out.

- Stephen Covey

159. Great leaders are almost always great simplifiers, who can cut through argument, debate, and doubt to offer a solution everybody can understand.

- General Colin Powell

160. Great leaders are not defined by the absence of weakness, but rather by the presence of clear strengths.

- John Zenger

161. He who has great power should use it lightly.

- Seneca

162. He who has learned how to obey will know how to command.

- Solon

163. I cannot give you the formula for success, but I can give you the formula for failure, which is: Try to please everybody.

- Herbert Swope

164. If you would not be forgotten, as soon as you are dead and rotten, either write things worth reading, or do things worth the writing.

- Benjamin Franklin

165. In matters of style, swim with the current; in matters of principle, stand like a rock.

- Thomas Jefferson

166. It is absurd that a man should rule others, who cannot rule himself.

- Latin Proverb

167. It is better to lead from behind and to put others in front, especially when you celebrate victory when nice things occur. You take the front line when there is danger. Then people will appreciate your leadership.

- Nelson Mandela

168. Lead and inspire people. Don't try to manage and manipulate people. Inventories can be managed but people must be led.

- Ross Perot

169. Leadership cannot just go along to get along. Leadership must meet the moral challenge of the day.

- Jesse Jackson

170. Leadership is a potent combination of strategy and character. But if you must be without one, be without the strategy.

- Norman Schwarzkopf

171. Leadership is solving problems. The day soldiers stop bringing you their problems is the day you have stopped leading them. They have either lost confidence that you can help or concluded you do not care. Either case is a failure of leadership.

- Colin Powell

172. Management is efficiency in climbing the ladder of success; leadership determines whether the ladder is leaning against the right wall

- Stephen Covey

173. Never give an order that can't be obeyed.

- General Douglas MacArthur

174. No man is good enough to govern another man without that other's consent.

- Abraham Lincoln

175. One of the tests of leadership is the ability to recognize a problem before it becomes an emergency.

- Arnold Glasow

176. The final test of a leader is that he leaves behind him in other men, the conviction and the will to carry on.

- Walter Lippman

177. The growth and development of people is the highest calling of leadership.

- Harvey Firestone

178. To do great things is difficult; but to command great things is more difficult.

- Friedrich Nietzsche

179. To have long term success as a coach or in any position of leadership, you have to be obsessed in some way.

- Pat Riley

180. True leadership lies in guiding others to success. In ensuring that everyone is performing at their best, doing the work they are pledged to do and doing it well.

- Bill Owens

181. We live in a society obsessed with public opinion. But leadership has never been about popularity.

- Marco Rubio

182. Whatever you are, be a good one.

- Abraham Lincoln

183. You gain strength, courage and confidence by every experience in which you really stop to look fear in the face. You must do the thing you think you cannot do.

- Eleanor Roosevelt

184. A competent leader can get efficient service from poor troops, while on the contrary an incapable leader can demoralize the best of troops.

- John J Pershing

185. A good leader is a person who takes a little more than his share of the blame and a little less than his share of the credit.

- John Maxwell

186. There are three essentials to leadership: humility, clarity and courage.

- Fuchan Yuan

187. I am endlessly fascinated that playing football is considered a training ground for leadership, but raising children isn't.

- Dee Dee Myers

188. My responsibility is getting all my players playing for the name on the front of the jersey, not the one on the back.

- Unknown

189. A good plan violently executed now is better than a perfect plan executed next week.

- George Patton

190. The supreme quality of leadership is integrity.

- Dwight Eisenhower

191. Earn your leadership every day.

- Michael Jordan

192. The greatest leader is not necessarily the one who does the greatest things. He is the one that gets the people to do the greatest things."

- Ronald Reagan

193. Becoming a leader is synonymous with becoming yourself. It is precisely that simple and it is also that difficult."

- Warren Bennis

194. Remember the difference between a boss and a leader; a boss says "Go!" - a leader says "Let's go!"

- E.M. Kelly

195. A chief is a man who assumes responsibility. He says "I was beaten," he does not say "My men were beaten."

- Antoine de Saint-Exupery

196. A leader leads by example, whether he intends to or not.

- Author Unknown

197. Leadership is action, not position.

- Donald H. McGannon

198. You can't lead anyone else further than you have gone yourself.

- Gene Mauch

199. The leadership instinct you are born with is the backbone. You develop the funny bone and the wishbone that go with it.

- Elaine Agather

200. You don't have to hold a position in order to be a leader.

- Anthony J. D'Angelo

201. Leaders are visionaries with a poorly developed sense of fear and no concept of the odds against them.

- Robert Jarvik

(Contd. Collection of Quotes)

My second book **Unique Quotes on Leadership and Management** is the best collection of more than 1000 quotes given by the most inspiring and successful people and some of the world's best minds

Apart from this it also covers the topics of leadership lessons that can be learnt from animals and birds (inspiring leadership stories and quotes learnt from eagles, Dove, Pigeon, elephants, ants other birds and animals)

Leadership quotes on Management

Leadership quotes on emotional intelligence

Leadership quotes from famous political and historical figures

Leadership quotes from military leaders

Fun filled leadership quotes

Leaders words of Wisdom

Leadership quotes on teamwork, business collaboration, culture and management

Leadership quotes on empathy and communication

Leadership quotes on effectiveness doing the right thing

Leadership quotes on bad Leadership (Leader vs Boss vs Manager)

Leadership quotes on Being a True Leader and example

Leadership quotes on having a vision, innovation and dreams, the future

Inspiring Leadership stories and quotes from Eagles, Dove, Pigeon, Elephants and other birds and animals

****

9 789354 277214

Printed by Libri Plureos GmbH in Hamburg,
Germany